UPMINSTER

The Story of a Garden Suburb

UPMINSTER

The Story of a Garden Suburb

TONY BENTON
WITH ALBERT PARISH

AMBERLEY

First published in 1996 by Tony Benton

This edition published 2009

Amberley Publishing Plc
Cirencester Road, Chalford
Stroud, Gloucestershire, GL6 8PE

www.amberley-books.com

British Library Cataloguing in Publication Data.
A catalogue record for this book is available from the British Library.

ISBN 978 1 84868 382 2

Typesetting and origination by Amberley Publishing
Printed and bound in Great Britain

CONTENTS

Greetings from UPMINSTER.

ST. LAWRENCE CHURCH.

BROADWAY.

THE MILL.

YEW AVENUE LEADING TO CHURCH.

CORBETS TAY.

ACKNOWLEDGEMENTS

I WOULD LIKE TO thank all those who have helped in some little way during my researches over the past few years and in particular:

The late George Aggiss; Mrs Ruth Davis; the late Hugh Drake; Mrs Gladys Ellis; Miss Joan Hills; Miss Mary Killingback; the late Keith Martin; Mrs Gill Plater; Mrs Ivy Pratt; John Roome; Miss Madeline Salinger; the late Doug Westrop; and also the staff of Romford Reference Library and the Essex Record Office.

The following are also thanked for supplying photos found on the following pages:

Mrs Ruth Davis (17, 40, 46, 66 and 89); London Borough of Waltham Forest (19 - bottom); Mrs B Bland (21); Mrs Gladys Ellis (97, 105, and 130); Miss Joan Hills (36, 76 and 154); the late Keith Martin (54); the late George Aggiss (103); Miss Madeline Salinger (67); Gaynes School (78and 105); the late Albert Parish (83, 93, 98 and 144); John Roome (106 and 107); Essex Record Office (103); and Mrs Anne Finch (98).

AUTHOR'S PREFACE

N O DOUBT THERE are many who think it was a very easy matter to write a sort of preface to such a singular, insignificant, and unworthy book as this is, but as there has been certainly not a little trouble involved, and necessarily so, in getting together the various constituent elements, or items, of which it is composed, so also there is some little difficulty in writing anything likely to be useful or accepted in the shape of a prefatory note, or argument, in reference to its content . . .

Thomas Lewis Wilson
27 December 1893
(Essex Record Office T/P 67/2)

T.L. Wilson's words of a century or more ago, despite their evidently Victorian use of language, convey the sentiments of any local historian who treads the ground where others have gone before. The bibliographical notes at the end of this book confirm that there has been no shortage of books about Upminster, from Wilson's own original history to a recent pictorial history and a book which includes a former resident's youthful memories. Why then another book on Upminster?

As my interest in Upminster developed about four years ago I realised that what had been written to date, for a variety of reasons dealt mainly with Upminster as it used to be with very little attention paid to how Upminster came to be developed since the early years of this century. Although the key points had been recorded, the story had not been told in the same detail that Upminster's earlier history had been covered. I therefore decided to find out more and to set it down in the form of a modern history.

My interest in local history grew from my interest in family history and I like to think this book reflects this. I have tried to tell the story as it developed for the people of Upminster who have no doubt mostly shared my indifference to the intricacies of local government administration which still attract much attention from local historians. In any event this aspect has been dealt with well before, as has the history of buildings, past and present. Neither have I tried to make this an assembly of people's memories, although I have drawn on oral history in many cases. This book has involved a considerable amount of first-hand research, much in contemporary newspapers. This has allowed me to provide exact dates for events, which in some cases conflict with earlier accounts, some well known. The Bibliographical Notes give more detail about many of the sources used but if anyone wants a specific reference or evidence for anything in this book please contact me.

To many people in and around London, Upminster perhaps signifies 'the end of the line', as it marks the easternmost terminus on London underground's District Line. (Indeed *The End of the Line* had been suggested to me as a possible title, one I rejected as being too negative.) But to numerous others Upminster remains a suburb which many people progressing up the ladder in Havering and beyond aspire to move to. For those who have grown up in Upminster, or who have managed the desired house move, Upminster remains a very pleasant place to live, with the advantages of closeness to London but ready access to the Essex countryside. But these relative newcomers and many residents of longer standing alike may know very little about how the development of Upminster was shaped during the first half of this century and the events and people who contributed to this process. This book aims to fill this gap.

Tony Benton, Upminster, October 1996

PREFACE TO THE 2009 EDITION

It's difficult to believe that it's almost thirteen years since *Garden Suburb* was published and about ten years since it's been in print. I'm delighted that Amberley Publishing have now decided to produce this new edition which is a big improvement on the original self-published edition.

That edition was very much a personal labour of love, and I've taken the opportunity to correct minor errors and typos that crept into the original, as well as rewording some sections where I felt the 1996 prose needed some improvements. I've also replaced some of the original photos with similar, better images as my collection has grown considerably in the years since then.

What I have not done is attempt to update the text to cover the many changes since 1996, particularly to Station Road Traders – the most recently announced being the sale of the Roomes Fashion and Homes Store to Morley Stores.

Hopefully this new edition will be appreciated by those who read it the first time round, as well as by a new audience – including the many newcomers who continue to be attracted by Upminster as a great place to live.

For those who may wonder what's coming next, my current researches will hopefully result in a 'prequel' to this book, the story of Upminster in the Victorian period, before the Garden Suburb was built. As ever, if anyone has any information or photographs about old Upminster please get in touch with me.

INTRODUCTION

F ROM EARLIEST TIMES Upminster relied on farming, both arable and
pasture to support much of its workforce, together with the employment
of estate workers and domestic servants in its manors and larger houses. Sheep
and cattle passed through Upminster and its neighbour Hornchurch on the well-
established route to the cattle market at Romford. The drover and his dog usually
maintained full control of the sheep despite the temptation of the lush grass
alongside the hedges bordering Upminster Road and Hornchurch Road. The
two villages were then entirely separate communities with open farmland and
meadows dividing them.

On weekday late afternoons farm wagons left regularly for Covent Garden
Market, which was the outlet for agricultural produce. The driver's dog trotted
between the rear wheels, his guard duties only ceasing in the early hours of the
following morning when the wares were unloaded and placed in the hands of
market wholesalers. His reward was a sleep on the long journey home on a
warm rug alongside the driver, who also nodded off more than not, secure in the
knowledge that his horse knew the way and would complete the journey home
to the farmyard gate.

The above was written earlier this year by the late Albert George Parish. In
February 1915 when Albert was born in Hornchurch, six months after the start
of the war with Germany, these scenes were still an everyday feature. When
Albert left school in 1930 and came to work for Gates and Son in Upminster's
Station Road the same might just about be said, although within a few years
'the open farmland and meadows' between Hornchurch and Upminster would
give way to bricks and mortar. Today, it is difficult to believe that these words
were true within living memory.

This book owes much to Albert Parish and, as agreed with him, his name
appears alongside mine in the title. His knowledge of Upminster, acquired
by his personal involvement of the events of the past sixty-five years, was

unrivalled. With his unexpected and untimely death on 11 March 1996 a massive store of memories has been lost. I am very pleased that he was able to work so closely with me in committing to paper many of those experiences. I know that it gave him pleasure to recall times past and to set these down for posterity. This book is therefore dedicated to his memory.

In terms of the division of labour, Albert's major contributions were to the two long chapters on Station Road Traders, and to the chapter on the 1930s and he also provided detailed comments and input on the Second World War chapter. All of Albert's contributions distil his unique and personal memories of people, places and events.

A horse-drawn cartload of hay and its driver on their way past Upminster Bridge heading towards Hornchurch around 1910. Already speculative building has started to encroach on the route but it was only in the 1930s that development was completed.

1

THE COMING OF THE RAILWAYS

THURSDAY 11 OCTOBER 1883 was a day of some importance and excitement for the parish of Upminster and its people. At noon that day a distinguished party left Fenchurch Street by train, transferring at Rainham Station to seven four-horse coaches which brought them to Upminster. Here they were met by the 'leading gentry of the neighbourhood' and villagers who gave them a 'hearty welcome' and accompanied them to a hilltop just north of Upminster windmill where the ceremonial cutting of the first turf of the Barking to Pitsea extension of the London, Tilbury and Southend Railway was to be performed. After a blessing and prayer from the Rector of Chadwell (the Rev. A.E. Clementi-Smith) Mr Arthur L. Stride, engineer and general manager of the company, invited Mrs Doughty Browne, the Chairman's wife, to turn the first sod, using the silver spade and 'miniature barrow of walnut' presented by Mr W.H. Knight of the contractors Kirk and Parry. This she did 'in a very graceful manner' amid 'hearty cheers' from the onlookers, before the party retired to the refreshment tents and further speeches.

Upminster had been chosen as the venue as a ceremony, rather than the existing railway towns of Barking or Pitsea, as either of these places would not have held the same significance. But this occasion, although similar to many others held throughout the Victorian period, was notable as many outside observers felt that the coming of the railroads to Upminster undoubtedly would unlock the door to the development of the most eligible parish in Essex. By popular assent Upminster and the surrounding district was 'capable of considerable development as a place of residence'. In the speeches that followed the turf-cutting ceremony, Mr Doughty Browne, the railway company's chairman, 'expressed the hope that a large residential traffic would be developed' while the engineer Mr Stride hoped that by 'judicious regulations and by excluding the "jerry-builder"' the district would not be ruined as had other picturesque localities. To the reporter from the *Essex Times* 'it would be more difficult to find a more charming district, and there can be no question that it would have been selected as a site for high-class residential property had not the means of communication with the metropolis been so poor'. In his view, now that the 'disadvantage' of Upminster's 'remoteness from the iron roads' was about to be overcome, the beauty of the area would 'tempt people to live there *if they could*'. Although the reporter did not realise it, his choice of words was to prove apt: it was to be over twenty years before people in significant numbers 'could' meet their desire to live there. The fact was that land for development did not become openly available in the same way that it had elsewhere on London's blossoming suburban fringe. As a result the expectations of the London, Tilbury and Southend Railway Company's chairman, and the return on the company's investment, were not to be realised for several decades.

Looking east along Upminster Broadway towards Cosy Corner, the Bell Inn and Eldred's Forge, 1880.

Among the dignitaries gathered on the Upminster hilltop on that Thursday afternoon in October 1883 was the striking figure of Thomas Lewis Wilson, who two years previously had further raised his already-high local profile by issuing his *History and Topography of Upminster*, an updated version of his earlier parish history. In addition to his antiquarian and historical interests Wilson was in all ways a man of many parts: builder, brick and tile manufacturer, contractor, and undertaker – amongst other things – as well a loyal and faithful member of Upminster's Congregational Church. Indeed had it not been for his staunch nonconformist principles and the deep-seated and long-standing personal animosity between him and Upminster's Rector, the Rev. Phillip M. Holden, he would have added to his talents by taking a more prominent role in parish affairs. But as it was his future civic service as member of the inaugural Upminster Parish Council lay over ten years in the future. Despite his antiquarian leanings Wilson could in no way be viewed as one rooted in the past, wishing to see no change in his home parish. In fact the opposite is true, for his business interests ensured that he would be well-placed to profit when the sought-after development of the parish eventually got under way and Wilson was one of those most vociferous in calling for Upminster to be developed.

Born in 1833, Wilson had celebrated his fiftieth birthday by the time that the turf-cutting ceremony was held. Eight years previously, in 1875, he had taken over the family carpentry and undertaker's business in Cranham Road, now St Mary's Lane (opposite the current junior school) on the death of his father, Thomas Wilson senior. In keeping with his wide-ranging interests Wilson diversified his business, entering a partnership with Edward Hook, which was to last some thirty years, collaborating on a variety of building ventures, including for a time lessees of the brick kiln and works in Bird Lane, making bricks, tiles and pipes. Wilson's interest in, enthusiasm for and initial information about the local parish history had been acquired from his father Thomas, who clearly did not fit the usual mould of a village carpenter and builder. This interest led him to build up a collection of newspaper cuttings and other documents which offered some insight into parish life as it happened or as it was in earlier years. In 1856, when just twenty-three years old, Thomas junior published his first parish history *Sketches of Upminster*, an updated and finely illustrated version of which was published twenty-five years later as *History and Topography of Upminster*. Wilson's contribution to recording Upminster's history is invaluable, for not only did he produce these two read-able studies about the local area but from 1880 until just before his death in 1919 he also kept a series of scrapbooks holding his collection of cuttings, documents and jottings, some fourteen bulky volumes in all, now preserved for reference at the Essex Record Office, Chelmsford.

To the visitors and local dignitaries at the hilltop ceremony the scene 'com-manded a view which excited the admiration of all and the astonishment of not a few of the visitors'. The party's hilltop vantage point was, at most, barely 100ft above sea level yet it offered a view of much of Upminster and on a clear day the hills on the south side of the river could be seen; occasionally the Crystal Palace at Sydenham was a noticeable feature. Indeed it was similar to the 'bird's-eye view' from the top of the windmill described by Wilson two years earlier:

> Beneath us are two roads, crossing each other in the direction of the cardinal points, the church, the chapel, the schools, and a few dwellings in the village. The grounds of Gaines are seen in the south, with Hacton to the right and Fox Hall on the left; Upminster Hall and Manor in the north, New Place in the east

and Bridge House in the west. The features of our neighbouring parishes and of the country many miles round are distinctly visible from this elevation, which commands a panorama of forty miles diameter from east to west, exhibiting that pleasing interspersion of fields, and woods, and homesteads, which is so general in our part of the country, encircled by the hills of Middlesex, Surrey and Kent, and more beautiful than our villagers imagine.

Certainly, the narrow width of the parish, no more than one mile in extent at any point and little more than half-a-mile wide at the village centre, ensured that the east-west perspective was in view. To the west the spire of St Andrew's parish church in Hornchurch and the nearby Hornchurch windmill were prominent across the Ingrebourne valley; to the east the low hills around Laindon were in sight.

From where the group stood the parish sloped gently southwards to a height of 50ft above sea level on the Thames flood plain. One mile south of the village centre was the large hamlet of Corbets Tey, at this time supporting three public houses, but contracting in size with two of these hostelries closing before the end of the nineteenth century. In Upminster's southern part, well-drained and fertile loam masked a deep layer of Thames gravel and sand, forming what Wilson termed 'the turnip and barley lands of the parish'.

Upminster's windmill framed a southern aspect of a near-idyllic country village set around a crossroads, often referred to as the 'Four-Wantz Corner'. In this area – the 'nursery of the parish' – the lands were friable with fertile brick-earth, which was 'very productive, and well adapted to the growth of every species of corn and vegetables'. Here were concentrated many of the population together with the bulk of the features described by Wilson: the parish church of St Laurence; the well-attended Congregational chapel on Upminster Hill,

Upminster cross-roads from the tower of St Laurence's Church, 1907.

west of the village centre; and the National School, with its attached school-house and distinctive turret, and the British School, which stood opposite each other in Hall Lane (soon to be called Station Road), about to be unwillingly brought together under a local School Board. Northwards from the hilltop, the uplands rose gradually, reaching their 'peak' of around 250ft at Warley Street, by Upminster (Tylers) Common. Close to here at Bird Lane lived a small working community employed on the brickfields and on local farms, where the combination of soils – a thin loam resting on the stiff London clays, with pockets of brickearth, sand and gravel – made cultivation expensive.

The road pattern had little altered since the eighteenth century or earlier. Crossing

from west to east were three roads: in the centre running from Hornchurch to Cranham was St Mary's Lane, although at this time the part west of the village centre was known as Upminster Hill or Hornchurch Road, while the eastern part was commonly referred to as Cranham Lane; to the north Shepherds' Hill ran from Harold Wood along the south side of the common, continuing eastwards into Great Warley parish as Warley Road; while south of the village centre Hacton Lane ran southwards, becoming Aveley Road and forming the boundary with the southerly neighbouring parishes of Aveley and Rainham. The long six-mile north-south axis was bisected along much of its length by a single route entering the parish from South Weald as Nags Head Lane in the north, crossing the common and running downhill towards the

Hall Lane, near the junction with Bird Lane.

village as Hall Lane, taking its name from the manor house of Upminster Hall. From the village centre the route continued southwards as Corbets Tey Road, the main road swinging eastwards at Corbets Tey hamlet running on past Stubbers House towards North Ockendon in the east, while westwards from the hamlet Harwood Hall Lane ran to join Aveley Road. Other minor routes which reached Hall Lane and its southern extension were Bird Lane, which joined Hall Lane to Warley Road in the north, and Little Gaynes Lane, which ran west from Gaynes

Cross on Corbets Tey Road past Gaynes manor house to join with Hacton Lane and Hornchurch parish.

After the hilltop opening ceremony in October 1883, no time was lost in starting work on the railway extension, working eastwards from Barking. But when the excavations reached Upminster in March 1884 there was some anxiety in the local population. Henry Joslin Esq. of Gaynes hosted a 'Navvies Tea' attended by 130 of the railway constructors who dined on huge sausage rolls, bread and butter, tea and fruitcake and listened to Joslin's encouragement that they carry out their work without disruption to the locality. But despite these exhortations, the works were not without occasional controversy in the area. The crushing to death by a wagon of a well-known railway navvy, 'Cambridge George' Wilson in September 1884 cast a shadow on the forthcoming line, while there was bad odour four months later in January 1885 when a gang of over 100 'stalwart navvies were in full swing, apparently forgetful of the fact that it was a Sunday'.

In contrast to the inaugural turf cutting in October 1883, as planned rail services connecting Upminster with the London, Tilbury & Southend Company's Fenchurch Street terminus, via Barking, were opened without ceremony just over eighteen months later on 1 May 1885. Only a few enthusiasts travelled out of curiosity on the first of the daily service, starting with the 7.13 am, which cost from 11*d* for a third class single to 3*s* for a first class return. The new service provided Upminster with fifteen trains a day to Fenchurch Street, with

Upminster Station, opened 1 May 1885, provided the parish with direct links to London's Fenchurch Street terminus.

stops at Hornchurch, Dagenham and Barking. Even though the station buildings were not completed when the line opened when the station at Upminster
was finally finished it was seen to be 'almost identical with Dagenham but on
a larger scale'. There was a subway 'faced with white glazed bricks' together
with a 'large number of sidings, engine shed, coal stage and water cranes'.

Three years later in February 1888 it was still 'a matter of some surprise' to
the *Essex Weekly News* that 'no signs are yet apparent of those first class country villa residences for which there is so great a demand'. Even if building was
not yet in evidence the countryside was at least accessible to visitors. On Bank
Holidays hundreds used the railway connections to visit Upminster for the day:
the 'picturesqueness of the village' being 'sufficient attraction in itself'.

Although it seems never to have become public knowledge, the Branfill
family were spurred by the building of the railway to consider developing a
housing estate on that part of their Upminster Hall estate, which had been
isolated from the main estate by the new railway line. As early as January
1886, a detailed plan of the area south of the railway and east of Station
Road was prepared for Capt. Benjamin Aylett Branfill by the family's architects Chancellors of Chelmsford. This envisaged a 'Railway Road' running
roughly parallel to the London, Tilbury & Southend railway – similar to the
route adopted for Howard Road twenty years later – and 'Champion Road',
approximately along the line of the current St Lawrence Road. Another proposed road ran south from Railway Road across the end of Champion Road,
joining St Mary's Lane opposite the Clockhouse/New Place – the route later
adopted for Garbutt Road. Branfill tried variations on this plan on several
occasions over the next fifteen years but presumably lacked the finances or
failed to attract a developer interested in the plans.

But in the meantime, even if housing developments were not forthcoming,
other limited signs of progress had been unavoidable. On the night of 1/2 August
1888 the River Ingrebourne overflowed its banks, with water running over
the bridge and deluging the adjacent Bridge House Inn on the Hornchurch-
Upminster road and cutting two long channels, 5 ft deep on the Hornchurch side.
The need for a new bridge was recognised and in December 1891 a new and
improved bridge was opened over the River Ingrebourne over twice the width of
its predecessor. Wilson had a bright idea: to seal into the brickwork a 'stoneware
receptacle' containing copies of coins, local newspapers, photographs and other
items, including a copy of Wilson's book autographed by local residents, to give
future generations an impression of nineteenth-century life.

In addition to the improved access to Hornchurch which the bridge provided
other improvements came in May 1889 when telegraphic communications reached
Upminster for the first time. By early 1890 work on the Romford to Grays railway
route was under way although this was not without problems – wagon fillers on
the Upminster-Grays section came out on strike for increased pay in February

1891, although the strike collapsed after a few days with a return to work. On 1 July 1892 the rail link between Upminster and Grays, single-track with a passing loop at South Ockendon, was opened. Less than a year later on Wednesday 7 June 1893 the rail line to Romford completed the railway network in the area. There was no formal public opening and just twenty-nine passengers in addition to the railway officials travelled on the first train, the 6.58 am to Romford. The initial service comprised of eight trains each way, with three extra on Saturdays and five each way on Sundays. According to the Essex Times 'the rail facilities of Upminster were now second to those of no other place within a radius of miles'.

Upminster's water supply, mainly provided by the abundant local springs, had been supplemented by the South Essex Waterworks' mains which passed through on their route from Romford to Grays. Nevertheless, drainage continued to present

Above: Looking towards Upminster past the Bridge House Inn and across the enlarged Upminster Bridge, 1904.

Right: The new railway cutting between Upminster and Grays, July 1890.

a problem owing to the geography of the parish, and it was only in 1893, after threat of prosecution, that the drainage authority, the Romford Rural sanitary authority, piped the Cranham Road (St Mary's Lane) ditch. This was only a limited improvement and during 1894 a petition with 4,400 names led to a public enquiry into the need for drainage in the parish. But it was to be five more years – and nine years since the first complaint – before the parish was provided with mains sewage, although this was confined to the village and Corbets Tey.

At the end of 1894 came the election of the first parish council by show of hands, without a formal poll. Nineteen candidates offered themselves for election to the new council of nine members which, as a newspaper noted, comprised 'chiefly the leisured and trading classes'. The successful members who formed the new body were: Mr Isaac M. Gay, farmer of Great Sunnings, 103 votes; Frank Rowe, plumber (and later publican of the Huntsman and Hounds, 101; The Rev. A.M. Carter, 94; E. Brown, gentleman, 88; Thomas L. Wilson, builder etc (and Upminster's historian), 87; Richard Clark, timber merchant, 82; Mr E. Sydney Woodiwiss, gentleman of Hill Place, 82 votes; George West, schoolmaster, 79; and Henry Deering, boot and shoemaker, 69. Henry Joslin of Gaynes was among those who failed to gain election, registering only 56 votes.

But despite these limited signs of progress little else had changed in the village. The Essex 'character' Spurgeon, scornfully considered that Upminster remained 'a landmark by the wayside where we periodically pull up and take stock of the situation as we march down the streets of Time'. From a different perspective, the *Christian World* in 1897 remarked how it was 'really exceptional to come across a village that, whilst proud of its beauty and rural charm, is at the same time anxious to avoid publicity lest the speculative builder should seize on its prey'. It was still 'almost entirely unknown and where scarce a modern house is to be seen'.

But lack of publicity was not entirely the cause, for as the *Kent & Essex Globe* noted in October 1899 'land has been very difficult to obtain for building purposes owing to the old inhabitants being loath to sell their freehold, and also owing to a very large portion of land north of the line being entailed and therefore only to be obtained on lease'. But to some commentators at least the development of part of the Foxhall estate opposite Gaynes Park in early 1899 suggested that inroads were at last being made. The resultant building of Freshfields, bought by Mr W.G. Horncastle who 'removed from West Ham Park', was, however, hardly typical of the type of development likely to make an impact on the area. This large house had stabling for two horses, a coach house and harness room, together with tennis and croquet lawns, a vinery and a three-quarter acre paddock – hardly the type of house that speculative builders would have in mind when developing Upminster. Neither was the building from March 1905 of the grand Upminster Court mansion with its 22 acres of grounds to the west of Hall Lane for Mr Arthur E. Williams, a director of Samuel Williams

& Co., the shipping and coalhandler contractors, to the designs of a
Charles Reilly, owner of High House in Corbets Tey Road.

Yet Upminster's resistance to 'the march of progress' was slowly crumbli
1901, following the death of Col. Brydges Branfill, ten acres of the Mavisb
estate, which ran northwards from Upminster Hill at the east of the windmill, w
acquired by James Everett Dowsing and Samuel Davis, contractors of Mawney
Road, Romford with the intention of building Upminster's first major housing
development. At long last Wilson reaped the reward for his years of critical opposition to those who stood in the way of development: he received the instruction
to lay out the estate into building plots. Before long it was reported that 'roads,
sewers, kerbing and so on are being rapidly constructed', the lines of Gaynes
Road, Branfill Road and Champion Roads had been laid out for development on
what was described as the 'very appropriate name' of the Branfill Park Estate. But
over the next few years progress was slow with only limited numbers of houses
erected, just twenty-four by 1909. The largest number were on the south side of
Gaynes Road (currently Nos. 5-23) built in 1904 and 1905, with the remaining
development confined to several plots in Champion and Branfill Roads.

According to a 1905 press report Upminster was 'at last awakening to a
sense of its importance as a desirable residential quarter . . . and considering
the exceptional facilities of the place for railway travelling in all directions,
the salubrity of its air and its elevated situation, Upminster will doubtless soon
be the scene of much more extended operations in the building line . . . The
exigencies of trade and commerce within a short distance all round are so
continually pressing that they cannot in all cases be resisted much longer'.

And so it was to prove.

The south side of Gaynes Road on Dowsing and Davis's 'Branfill Park Estate' (on the left of the
picture) had been completed by 1905. The north side was later built by W.P. Griggs & Co.

2

ᴸS OF ELM AND OAK

ᴸNSTER, AN EDWARDIAN GARDEN SUBURB

T HE CLOSING YEARS of Queen Victoria's reign were marked by a housing boom to cater for the rapidly increasing population. Thousands of acres of countryside surrounding London gave way to serried ranks of almost identical red-brick terraced houses, typically unimaginative in layout, with long, straight streets on a grid-iron pattern which met the minimum conditions for frontage and size set down in by-laws. Trees and hedgerows were rooted up and all traces of the rural past were obliterated as estates were rapidly developed by speculative builders to meet what they felt were the needs of the blossoming lower-middle classes — the clerks, shop workers, teachers, salesmen and others who played an increasingly important role in Victorian society. But by the end of the queen's long reign there was increasing awareness and concern about the irreparable damage to the environment caused by this unplanned suburban growth. Many people were also starting to realise that the quality of life in the new suburbs left much to be desired. As *The Times* noted in 1904:

> to surround London with acres of such streets is to produce a district of appalling monotony, ugliness and dullness. And every suburban extension makes existing suburbs less desirable ... It is the more necessary, if possible, to redeem the suburb from meanness and squalor.

Another factor was at work: the rising hopes and aspirations of those middle-class suburban occupiers who could afford something better than their dull terrace and who wished to break away from rubbing shoulders with the working classes, from whose ranks many of them had emerged. In contrast to suburban housing, homes for the professional and upper middle classes were marked by their variety and style: there was clearly a need for new ideas on suburban development which would meet the lower middle classes' aspirations and their ability to pay for a better type of house.

The concept which did most to meet these emerging needs was the
city movement which had gained much attention and enthusiastic s
since it came to the public eye with the publication in 1898 of Ebei
Howard's book *Garden Cities of Tomorrow*. Howard's vision was for de
opments of quality housing on a grand scale set within surroundings whi
retained as much as possible of the characteristics of the countryside whic
they replaced. He saw the garden city as being self-contained, with industrial
zones within walking distance of employees' homes. Unlike many visionaries
Howard lived to see his ideas put into practice: in 1903 almost 4,000 acres of
land were acquired by the newly-established Garden City Pioneer Company
at Letchworth in Hertfordshire where work started on housing laid out at
low densities of no more than eight to the acre to designs by the architects
Raymond Unwin and Barry Parker.

A smaller scale variant on the garden city was the garden suburb, based on
Howard's ideas for houses set within rural surroundings but without the need for
a self-contained community with its own industries. Those as-yet undeveloped
London outskirts, with easy rail access to the employment opportunities of the
city, which had avoided the late-nineteenth-century developers' attentions, were
obviously ripe for development as garden suburbs.

It was against this background that towards the end of September 1906 W.P. (Peter, later Sir Peter) Griggs announced his intention of laying out some 700 acres of the Upminster Hall Estate for building purposes in a development which 'would preserve its healthy and rural condition and would attract a desirable class of people to Upminster'. In an interview with the *Essex Times* Griggs expanded on his proposals which were fully in keeping with the garden city and garden suburb ideals. There would be 'no more than two or three residences per acre and many would

Sir Peter Griggs (1849–1920).

have a larger area on which one could have 50 or 100 fruit trees and grow all
vegetables.' Larger houses were planned on the north of the railway, while to the
south of the line 'quite apart from the residential portion, so as to preserve its
quietude and peace', it was proposed to locate 'business premises and the smaller
class of house, with the cottages'. The Building Committee of the Romford Rural

proposal for a development which would 'preserve
appearance of the property, planting trees in the
frontage and from 60 to 70 feet, with depths of
Co. sought the council's advice on 'a specification of
table and adequate to the rural requirements of what would
den suburb'.

development was ambitious. In addition to the initial estates
the railway, on the land which the Branfills had sought to develop
years previously, and the area north of the railway flanking the prestig-
Hall Lane, Griggs planned to develop westwards to the River Ingrebourne
and eastwards to the boundary with Cranham. A further phase of building
would extend northwards on the west side of Hall Lane, as far as Upminster
Court, continuing progressively beyond Williams' property in a development
which would have stretched from the Ingrebourne to the Cranham boundary
in the north, running right past the Hall Lane junction with Bird Lane and
beyond. If completed, this would have taken Upminster's built area from the
railway to past the current arterial road (A127), except for the land directly
around Upminster Hall.

Peter Griggs was already a developer of some renown, ranking only behind
Cameron Corbett in the development of Ilford and surrounding areas. By
1898 his firm, W.P. Griggs & Co. Ltd., in which he was ably supported by
William Garbutt Key, had acquired the 215 acre Cranbrook Park Estate, Ilford
between the Cranbrook Road and the River Roding and had erected substantial, if monotonous, houses in streets bearing impressive names such as
Kensington Gardens, De Vere Gardens, and Mayfair Avenue. A second Ilford
estate, the Central Park Estate around Valentines Road, followed after 1900.
The 'Cranbrook Park and Central Park Estates' in Ilford were publicised to
be 'without question the choicest positions in Ilford and surrounding districts.
Substantially-built residences are being erected'. Griggs himself took residence
at No. 7 The Drive, with his partner Key as his next door neighbour at No.
5 while at No. 9 lived the Rev. Charles Vine, long-time minister of the Ilford
Congregational church at which Griggs worshipped fervently.

Published accounts of Griggs' life record his birth in 'humble surroundings
in South Hackney' on 1 November 1853 and state that his father, John, died
when Griggs was seven years old, leaving his mother, Martha, to bring up the
family alone. Reportedly apprenticed to a Thames lighterman, later saving
hard to buy his own barge, which he was forced to give up, Griggs saved to
buy another and in time made enough money to allow him to leave the river.
To what extent is this account true?

The birth entry for William Peter Griggs reveals a discrepancy with the
published accounts. His birth took place at 123 Brick Lane, Bethnal Green on
1 November 1849 – four years earlier than the birth date Griggs later admitted

to and in a different place. He was the son of John Griggs, a cheesemonger of Buckinghamshire origins, and his wife Martha, née Catt, with an older sister Martha and a younger brother Phillip. What then of his father's premature death? The London *Post Office Directories* confirm John Griggs, cheesemonger at the Brick Lane address from 1850 to 1858, succeeded by Mrs Martha Griggs until 1878. The entry for John's death, aged fifty-two, on 30 September 1857, caused by chronic hepatitis, confirms that young William Peter was indeed seven at the time of his father's death.

According to a published account Griggs 'by dint of rigid economy managed to save sufficient to acquire a £500 vessel, paying £100 down and the remainder by instalments'. By his own account 'at the age of 30 . . . I had made and lost a fortune. I determined to start again, and I recovered myself, although it took me years to do it'. The extensive records of the Company of Watermen & Lightermen confirm brief details of Griggs' career as a lighterman on the River Thames. Bound as an apprentice for five years to William Gregory of Deptford in October 1869 at the relatively late age of nineteen, Griggs paid his dues to the company as a working lighterman for ten years from 1874 to 1884. The company's registers of barge owners indeed confirm that, only a few years after becoming a fully fledged lighterman, Griggs had become the registered owner of a barge, soon adding another. The records also show that by 1878 when he was still only twenty-eight years old, he had given up being a sole owner, taking instead a share in three barges as a joint owner, which he relinquished in 1885. This broadly confirms the published accounts and suggests that Griggs' involvement with the lighterage trade ended around 1885.

However, the background to Griggs' conversion from the lighterman and barge owner of 1884/85 to major housing developer in 1897 remain obscure, although an obituary suggested that he came to Ilford from Bexley in Kent around 1890. Before his major developments at Ilford it seems that he was involved with building works at Wanstead, Walthamstow and Leyton. But by all yardsticks he was the epitome of the 'self-made man', typical of the Victorian era, who by his own efforts had risen from lower middle-class surroundings to considerable wealth and social prominence – he was elected to Ilford Council in 1899 and to Essex County Council two years later. By the end of 1904 W.P. Griggs and Co. had already contributed some 2,000 homes to Ilford's development but he acknowledged that it had 'been very difficult to keep things going. The firm has to give even more to people in the shape of improvements to induce them to buy'.

Griggs & Co.'s proposed development of the Upminster Hall Estate found favour with the media: the *Essex County Chronicle* concluded that 'if park land must be handed over to the builder "a garden suburb" is much to be preferred to a London dormitory'. With the support from the local council and such endorsement in the press the way was clear for Griggs to seal the purchase of the initial 150 acres of land on which the first stage of his estate was to grow. On 1 November 1906 he paid £20,000 to Capel Aylett Branfill and John Arthur Capel Branfill, trustees of the late Captain Benjamin Branfill, to acquire land extending 920ft to the west side of Hall Lane north of the railway, shortly to be developed as Waldgrave (later spelt Waldegrave), Engayne, and later Ashburnham Gardens. Fields eastwards of Hall Lane were also acquired, to become Deyncourt, Courtenay and Ingrebourne Gardens, together with the 15 acres to the south of the railway down to Cranham Road, on which Branfill had proposed to build and on which St Lawrence, Howard and Garbutt Roads were now to be built following similar plans. The agreement with the trustees prevented Griggs from building any house on Hall Lane 'of less value than £400 prime cost', no house was to be erected north of the railway for 'less than £250 prime cost' while no timber could be cut down 'except as might be necessary for the formation of roads or such as might be deemed by the district council or other local authority to be dangerous'.

From 1906 the rural delights of Hall Lane progressively gave way to building development.

The first brick was laid just over two weeks later on 17 November 1906, with the earliest attentions being paid to the prestigious detached houses on Hall Lane and the south side of Waldegrave Gardens, to the designs of the company's architect Mr George Verlyck. Within six months Griggs' publicity machine was in swing. By early May 1907 the national newspapers carried advertisements for houses on 'a real garden suburb near London' where 'choice residences of varied designs are being erected on this Picturesque Estate, on

Newly-built houses in Cranham Lane (now St Mary's Lane) around 1908.

high ground with very large gardens'. Prices were from £395 to £1,145, with 999 years' leases or freehold purchase available. The premium prices were reserved for a few exclusive detached properties on Hall Lane but in general the larger double-fronted four and five-bedroom detached houses on Hall Lane and in the adjoining roads sold for between £750 and £900, while semi-detached houses north of the railway sold for between £350 and £500. In contrast the much smaller houses on St Lawrence and Howard Roads typically sold for between £230 and £240, with those on Cranham Road (Esdaile Terrace) for around £275.

For the practically minded Griggs extolled the virtues of the easy rail access, offering to provide rail timetables, while for the more romantically minded readers the advertisement quoted from Tennyson urging them:

> To change our dark Queen City, all her realm
>   Of sound and smoke
> For His clear heaven and these few lanes of elm
>   And whispering oak.

Griggs was ready to publicise his development in a big way. On 24 May 1907 a large party of newspaper reporters and others of influence gathered at Fenchurch Street Station where they were met by Griggs and his fellow director, Mr J.W. Thompson, MP for East Somerset. At Upminster the guests were able to witness the rapid progress of the past six months: between twenty and thirty 'very imposing' detached villas 'of commanding appearance' and other semi-detached properties were on view. The showpiece was perhaps Glen Caladh, (now 28 Hall Lane) to which W.G. Key had already moved from his Ilford home. Here the guests 'had an opportunity of forming an idea of the value of these handsome dwellings in the garden suburb' and were entertained with a 'capital luncheon', followed by speeches by Griggs, Thompson, Dr V. Rutherford, MP for Brentford, and Mr Holland, Chairman of the Woolwich Building Society. Universally good publicity in the local and national newspapers followed. According to the *Daily News* Upminster was 'one of the true beauty spots in an under-rated county' while the *Grays and Tilbury Gazette* described the houses as 'modern certainly, but artistically modern'. The *Civil Service Gazette* recommended that 'civil servants who contemplate living in the country should pay Upminster a visit' and felt that 'it is not too much to say that the first garden suburb worthy of the name bids well to prove an unqualified success'.

Progress continued unabated. The Rural District Council deliberated in December 1906 about plans for the sewers to serve the estate, and the necessary loan of £450 from the Public Works Loan Commission was finally approved over six months later. Mr F.C. Thompson was appointed as the council's contractor, starting work on 20 August 1907, and the sewer's course under the railway to the sewage works at Puddle Dock, Cranham was complete by late September, ready for connection to the estate.

By the start of July 1907 the road surface of Waldegrave Gardens had been hardened and portions of the footpath spread with gravel, and a few

Waldegrave Gardens, pictured here in 1908, was the first street whose maintenance responsibilities were accepted by the local Council.

Properties on Howard Road were 'a smaller class of house, with cottages' quite apart from those north of the railway.

weeks later the metalling of Hall Lane was under way. By early September the company reported that they had 'practically finished' making up Hall Lane, Waldegrave, Engayne and Deyncourt Gardens. The council surveyor had a different view: the road surface of Engayne Gardens was 'rough, the kerbs not properly jointed . . . and no gas lamps and columns have been provided' while both sides of the other streets had not been 'wholly built upon and all houses fully completed'. It was to be nearly eleven months before the council were prepared to accept that the roads were nearing the stage where the council would take over their maintenance. Waldegrave Gardens came first – the six months' period of maintenance by the company running from July 1908 to January 1909 when the council took it over as a public road – to be followed in May 1909 by lengths of Engayne, Deyncourt and Courtenay Gardens. The *Romford Recorder* felt that 'this speaks well for the progress that has been made by the owners of the garden suburb'.

Not all housing developments in Upminster ran as smoothly as Griggs' garden suburb development. A less than successful venture took place just across the border in Cranham where in early 1907 the Land Company, 68 Cheapside, EC1 initiated the sale by auction of plots on the 'Cranham Park Estate', around Moor Lane, Cranham Gardens and Park Avenue. It was claimed that this development would not only appeal to the investor but 'to the City Man or anyone else whose business is principally in the Metropolitan area but who desires to live in healthy country surroundings away from unending streets of bricks and mortar'. Although the Romford Rural Council had disallowed the scheme when it was submitted for approval in November 1907, in July 1908 the council's attention was drawn to the fact that streets had been laid out without permission. In December that year the council agreed to take proceedings against the Land Company as they had laid out streets without complying with local by-laws. The following year the District Medical Officer of Health noted with concern in his annual report that houses had already been built and others 'were being erected without proper water supply'; by 1911 he was able to report that the estate, which hitherto had depended 'for its water supply upon a neighbouring private source' had at last been connected to the South Essex Water Company's mains.

Meanwhile building work had also been proceeding rapidly from around 1906 on Griggs' estate to the south of the railway, with the initial stretches of Howard and St Lawrence Roads being developed eastwards from Station Road by 1907. By July 1911 the developments of smaller houses on both sides of these long roads, some 170 yards of Howard Road and 270 yards of St Lawrence Road, were complete and six months later the council accepted liability for their maintenance.

Griggs and Co.'s plans for development continued to expand, adding the New Place estate in September 1909 and, in the summer of 1911, the unfinished Branfill Park Estate was added to their land bank, immediately initiating proposals for future development. In May 1912 Griggs completed the purchase of a further 36 acres of the Upminster Hall Estate, directly to the east of Claremont Gardens.

The census of April 1911 recorded some 2,468 inhabitants in Upminster, an increase of almost one thousand or 60% on the 1901 total of 1,468 individuals. There were 553 families compared to 323 ten years earlier, suggesting that this first stage of Upminster's expansion had added around 230 houses, most in the four years since Griggs' development started in 1906.

Where then had Upminster's new residents come from? Large-scale evidence is lacking but some indication of residents' origins comes from the membership roll of the Upminster Congregational Church, which records details of those joining the church congregation and naming the church at which they had previously worshipped. This suggests that the largest group, headed by W.G. Key, had formerly lived in Ilford, possibly indicating that Griggs & Co. had targeted the residents of their other main developments. Forest Gate provided the next largest group, with others moving from nearby areas such as East Ham, Walthamstow, Leytonstone and Woodford. From further afield in Essex a small group had moved from Westcliff and Southend, attracted no doubt by a quicker daily rail journey to the city, while there appears to be some truth the *Civil Service Gazette*'s assertion that residents from 'all the better-class districts of London' were showing interest: among further-flung areas represented were Norwood and Muswell Hill.

Evidence of occupations for residents on the Upminster Hall Estate comes from the parish register: the earliest mentioned include bank clerk, schoolmaster, engineer, civil servant, retired manufacturer, Trinity House pilot, printer and draper – almost without exception solidly middle class. This was reinforced by the names of the houses. In Hall Lane the detached houses were given distinctive names including, in addition to Key's Glen Caladh, Daintree House, May Lodge, The Gables, The Croft, Broome Knowe; those named after trees such as The Pines, The Cedars, and The Elms; and those redolent of colonial origins, such as Kung Fah and Dilkusha. Houses on the Branfill Park Estate also bore grand titles such as Aldersmead, Valkyrie and Ellesmere in Champion Road and Ben Hilly and Lansdowne in Gaynes Road.

Courtenay Gardens was another of the streets built in Griggs' garden suburb from 1906 onwards.

3

A VILLAGE AT WAR

UPMINSTER 1914–18

D URING JULY 1914 escalating developments in Europe led Germany's declaration of war on France and the launching of an attack towards Paris, moving the German army through neutral Belgium. Britain had guaranteed Belgium's neutrality and after Germany declared war on that country, there was little option but for Britain to mobilise its forces, declaring war on Germany at midnight on 4 August 1914.

When the newly completed St Laurence church hall had opened on 17 April 1914, 'the result of a years labour', few would have guessed that within four months it would be pressed into emergency service as a hospital as part of the war effort. At the initiative of the rector, Rev. Hyla Holden, Dr John Storrs Brookfield, MD, of Hill Place, and 'a number of local ladies and gentlemen', within a few days of the outbreak of war a proposal was put forward to convert the new premises 'into a convalescent home for the care of men discharged from hospital', initially with twelve beds but with the capacity to expand to twenty beds if so required. The maintenance costs of £1 per bed per week were to be funded by pledges of help and public appeals, with Cranham parish prepared to do the whole of the laundry and provide a cook 'and other necessary services'; Dr Brookfield was to be the medical superintendent. An organised ambulance corps at Upminster station could provide 'two parties of bearers, with stretchers and equipment'. Evidently these proposals soon found favour with the necessary authorities.

Another early local response was the setting up of ladies' working parties to provide garments for troops. Shirts, bed jackets, helmets or sleeping caps, socks or mufflers and other items were assembled, with Miss Sophia Reilly of High House coordinating contributions. By the start of October 1914 some 400 garments had been made, some new, others adapted from old ones. The main beneficiaries were the 4th Battalion Essex Regiment who received a supply of helmets, shirts, socks, and mufflers, while other garments went to Upminster men serving with other regiments. Other clothes were sent to Purfleet camp, while about fifty articles were retained for use in the convalescent home in the church hall.

In the days running up to the announcement of hostilities and those which followed, men already in the regular forces or in the Territorial Reserve were drafted to form the first ranks of Britain's Expeditionary Force (BEF) or were called to arms and, as the parish magazine noted, Upminster men were involved from the outset. The BEF had been on the European mainland for less than a week when on 22 August the first casualty with Upminster connections occurred. The wounded man was Sergeant-Major D.S. Jillings, of No. 2 Squadron, Royal Flying Corps whose parents, Mr & Mrs A. Jillings, lived at Hill Place. Jillings was a regular soldier of some fourteen years service, having served in the Grenadier Guards until about twelve months previously.

But there were not enough regulars or reservists to take on the Kaiser's forces so volunteers were needed. A local recruitment office was soon established in Brook Street, Grays with the aim of recruiting 500 men from the surrounding districts. By 12 September the *Grays and Tilbury Gazette* was able to report that 312 men had enlisted but this included just four Upminster volunteers. But by 3 October at least nineteen men of Upminster from the Congregational Church alone were in uniform. The church sent a letter to each, 'expressing the good wishes of the church and a pocket New Testament, bound in khaki'. Three of the nineteen were to die on active service, the first (Leonard Cooper) perishing just seven months later in May 1915.

A better response was experienced following the call for special constables. By the end of September some seventy-two local men had been sworn in to 'defend' their parish, with seven more added the following week. These recruits were briefed 'as to their duties and what was required of them' and issued with armbands, whistles, truncheons and warrant-cards. The force paraded initially 'nearly every night at the railway station for drill' before taking up their nightly patrol duties around the parish. Like other places Upminster was swept with 'spy-mania' with the appearance of any stranger to the district met with suspicion and rumours. Anyone with a foreign or uncommon-sounding name came under the spotlight, including the long-established baker Mr Frizzell. To dampen down local sentiments, the rector found it necessary to write to the local paper urging his parishioners to be 'level-headed'. But the situation can hardly have been helped by the news at the end of October 1914 that Police Sergeant Beasley had arrested three Germans, who were shipped off to a transit camp at Newbury.

But the arrival of other foreigners in the area around the same time was cause for sympathy rather than concern. Belgian refugees, fleeing their invaded country, were welcomed warmly to Upminster and private houses in Gaynes Road were rented for them, funded by local donations. First-hand news about German atrocities against the Belgian people would have spread quickly in the village.

The shooting down of Zeppelin SL-11 at Cuffley by Lt Leefe Robinson was clearly visible from Upminster and surrounding areas.

The war must also have seemed closer to home with the announcement in early October that Private Charles Morant of the City of London Fusiliers was the first from the parish to be killed in action, dying in France on 10 September. The thirty year-old resident of Hacton hamlet was the first of over sixty men with parish links to perish in the conflict over the next four years.

When the war began in August the commonly held view was that it would be over by Christmas, but by Christmas Day there was firm evidence that the war was far from over. At lunchtime that day the sound of firing between British and German airplanes in the Thames estuary was heard in Upminster, and it was reported that the enemy had been fired upon in nearby Purfleet.

The war in the air began in earnest in spring 1915, particularly after 31 May 1915 when Zeppelin LZ-38 became the first airship to reach London. Living beneath a common German flight path the residents of Upminster would have sensed a constant threat to their safety. The British defences comprised a series of planes operating from airfields around the South East, a series of ground observation posts, with telephone contacts inland to relay warnings of the advancing threat, and mobile and fixed anti-aircraft batteries and searchlights. Locally these were to be found at Beacontree Heath in Dagenham, Buckhurst Hill and Chigwell Row, in addition to a searchlight station at Upminster Common. It was noted many years later that William Garbutt Key, Director of W.P. Griggs & Co., as Sergeant of the Special Constables and 2nd Essex Volunteer Regiment, transported men to this latter emplacement which the local volunteers manned for six months until it was taken over by the Royal Engineers.

Another local line of air defences came in October 1915 with the opening of Suttons Farm airfield in Hornchurch: early local action came on 13 October when an anti-Zeppelin patrol spotted airship L15 over Romford. On the night of 25/26 April 1916 a Zep was over Upminster, as an eyewitness who wrote to Finsbury Park recorded the next day:

> Yesterday... Woke up at 11pm by Mrs Brand all the household. Zep to be seen. Loud firing. Shells swizzing. Aeroplanes out etc. Bed 12.15pm. Did you hear anything?

The most dramatic incident in the locality was probably the occasion on the night of 2/3 September 1916 when Lt. Williams Leefe Robinson, flying out of Suttons Farm, became the first Allied airman to shoot down a German airship. Airship SL11 met its fate at his hands at Cuffley, Hertfordshire with the death of the commander and sixteen crew. The flames, said to be visible 40 or 50 miles away, would certainly have been seen at Upminster. Another incident came three weeks later with the shooting down of two Zeps in Essex at Great Burstead and Mersea Island. In neighbouring Hornchurch C.T. Perfect reported on the former's 'crimson glow, lighting up the country all around as it plunged earthwards'.

From spring 1915 onwards another dimension to the war was apparent with news of the ill-judged assault on the Gallipoli peninsular. The 1st Battalion Essex Regiment was amongst those involved in this disastrous campaign which cost 20,000 lives from April 1915, with two men with Upminster connections, Privates William Wenden and Arthur Hall, amongst that regiment's fatalities in the summer of 1915. Yet typically jingoistic accounts of the Gallipoli conflict appeared in the Upminster parish magazine and the local paper, penned by Private R.E. Newton of the 4th Essex Regiment, but it is unlikely that local people would have been easily fooled by this offering. The mounting casualty lists for the British forces meant that a constant supply of recruits was needed to replace these losses. Recruitment meetings, such as that held in Upminster on 20 November 1914, obviously played their part in calling men to arms, but the flow of volunteers alone was not enough to meet the demand. In July 1915 the National Registration Act compelled everyone between fifteen and sixty-five years of age to register, followed by a last chance to enlist voluntarily with the so-called 'Derby Scheme', introduced in October 1915 by Lord Derby. Those who chose not to volunteer could 'attest', with an obligation to come forward if called to do so. The scheme was to close on 15 December 1915, and in the week before this, from 9-11 December from 8 pm to 10 pm, a 'sub-recruiting office for attestation and enlistment' was opened at Upminster's British School. Lord Derby's report at the start of 1916 showed that by the closing date across the country just 215,000 men had volunteered for immediate service, with almost three million attesting. But still over one million males of military age had failed to register. The Military Service Act of January 1916 introduced compulsory military service for all single men aged eighteen to forty-one; an act four months later extended conscription to married men too. Only the medically unfit or those in essential ('starred') occupations were exempt. From 25 January 1916, unmarried eighteen to twenty-three year olds who had attested under the Derby arrangements were called up progressively over the next few months. Married attestees followed from March, along with conscripts in these age groups.

The war in Europe reached new horrors on 1 July 1916, the so-called first day of the Somme, when British soldiers were mown down in their thousands by the merciless German machine-gun fire. Among those regiments badly affected were the 10th Essex: two Upminster fatalities from that regiment were Pte Edward Butler, and L/Cpl Albion Caldecourt, son of John Richard Caldecourt, plumber, glazier and gas fitter of Elmhurst, Station Road (adjacent to A.E. Talbot's wheelwright's shop, later to be Talbot's garage). Caldecourt was an early volunteer, enlisting at Grays on 16 November 1914; his brother Frederick was to die in action two months later.

Jonathan Hills, a gardener at Gaynes Park, whose son Tom died as a result of his wounds.

A visible reminder of the war came in September 1916 with the military funeral in Upminster of Pte. Tom Hills, MM, a popular local figure. Hills had been born twenty-two years previously at Tadlows Cottages, where his parents Mr & Mrs Jonathan Hills, head gardener to Mr Joslin at Gaynes, still lived. Educated in the village schools, he became a choirboy, later following in his father's footsteps as a gardener and, after a period out of the district, returned to work at Gaynes. Unable to enlist in the army due to water on the knee, he gained a first-class ambulance certificate, subsequently enlisting in the Royal Army Medical Corps. He was fatally wounded on 9 September

1916 when attempting to reach a wounded man, having rescued one man already, and for his bravery under fire was awarded the Military Medal. He was sent back from the front to Netley Hospital, Southampton and managed to write a letter home to his parents but, before they could reach him, he passed away on 16 September, seven days after receiving his fatal wounds. Upminster parish church hosted his funeral with full military honours on 20 September, before the funeral procession of 'persons both civil and military, as well as several of the Upminster special constables' made its way to the cemetery at Corbets Tey.

As 1916 progressed, other tragic aspects of the war become evident to the people of Upminster as the effects of losing a loved one were keenly felt. A near neighbour of the Hills, Mrs Miles of Tadlows Cottage, received notice that her husband Edward, another of Joslin's employees at Gaynes Park whom she had married the previous Christmas Day, had been wounded on 19 July 1916 and was reported missing. By early October the *Grays and Tilbury Gazette* reported that she was still awaiting news of his fate, having advertised and written letter after letter to anyone she thought might have news. The official notice of his death came the following week. Mrs Coppen of Lynton Branfill Road also had to endure the anguish of waiting for news, in this case of her son, Bert (Herbert) Coppen of the 'Bankers' Battalion' (26th Royal Fusiliers). As the *Grays and Tilbury Gazette* reported on 3 November 1916: getting no further news of him seemed to prey on her mind to such an extent that she developed a brain fever… and passed away in St Thomas' hospital without practically regaining consciousness'. Almost exactly twelve months after her death, her eldest son Lt. William Coppen too was also killed in action.

Mr William J. Gooderham, a long-time resident who carried out the triple business as grocer, draper and postmaster to the parish, was another affected badly by the death of his son. Seven months after the death in November 1916 of Pte. John Gooderham of the Honourable Artillery Company after the capture of Beaumont Hamel, Gooderham circulated his customers with the news that 'owing to the sad loss I sustained last year, I have decided to dispose of my business … after twenty-six years', Mr A.W. Green of Ilford being the new owner. A lasting monument to John Gooderham, 'the gift of his parents', erected in October 1917, can still be seen in the east end of the Lady Chapel in St Laurence church: a stained glass window depicting the adoration of the Magi.

A new terror was inflicted on the skies above Upminster from May 1917 when daylight air raids were launched on London by flights of German Gotha bombers. Just before lunchtime on 13 June 1917 a flight of 14 Gothas, making their way westwards along the north banks of the Thames via Wickford, Brentwood, Romford and West Ham, were visible above the garden suburb. They 'were seen at a great altitude, appearing like whitish specks against the blue'. They were 'well to the north of the village and moving quickly' and

Station Road, Upminster.

After his son John was killed in action in 1916, W.J. Gooderham sold his three Upminster shops, including this one on the corner of Station Road and Howard Road.

out of sight in a few minutes. Upminster was left 'busied with conjectures as to what damage the visitors would do'. In fact the bombers inflicted heavy casualties in the capital – some 152 dead and 432 wounded – including the tragic death of 18 children at Upper North Street School, Poplar.

The nearby Suttons Farm airfield continued to play a major part in the air defences of Upminster and surrounding districts, with regular sorties against the invaders, although after the raids died out in 1917 and 1918 the base was used mainly as a gun emplacement. Towards the end of 1917 a re-organisation of the by-now Royal Air Force brought another aspect of the war to the people of Upminster: the newly-formed RAF 49 Wing, the administrative branch which commanded the local airfields of Suttons Farm, North Weald Basset and Hainault Farm, set up its HQ at Upminster Hall under Capt. Malcolm Christie. This development provided employment opportunities for local women who, in the absence of the bulk of the parish's menfolk, were recruited for service as cooks, drivers, clerks, typists, riggers and magneto repairers.

Despite many women's willingness to 'do their bit', not every man was keen to serve. In January 1917, William Thomas Pike, a thirty-eight-year-old married insurance clerk of Esdaile Gardens, was summonsed for failing to report when called up. He successfully claimed exemption on the grounds that he was a minister of the Upminster assembly of the Plymouth Brethren, whose assembly of around forty met in the former Congregational chapel on Upminster Hill. Most claims for exemption came from local employers, particularly shopkeepers like Mr Gooderham and his successor Green who consistently sought the exemption from service of their remaining key staff, a thirty-nine-year-old manager and thirty-one-year-old warehouseman and foreman, eight others having already left forward service. In August 1918 Bert Patience, private in the Essex Regiment, failed to report back for service: he was soon located at his parents' home in Corbets Tey and taken back to his unit. Increasingly men in the 'starred' occupations who had not volunteered for service found it necessary to appear before a military tribunal to justify their continued exemption. Sydney Abraham, who had been exempted as he worked for his namesake father in the Station Road bakers as dough maker and baker's boy, was passed for general service in March 1917.

One effect of the conscription of nearly all the adult males was that the social and sporting life of the parish virtually came to a halt. In the early war years many societies had managed to continue a restricted programme of events but as time went on even this became impossible. The Upminster Lawn Tennis Association formed in 1907, with their courts and pavilion in Deyncourt Gardens, 'became practically extinct' in 1917 'owing to the war and causes therefrom'. The club was re-established the following summer, when the end of the conflict was believed more likely.

Even as the war neared an end, news came of the deaths of more Upminster servicemen, not all as a direct effect of the enemy. Charles Arthur Riggall of Oak Cottage, Cranham Road was a sailor aboard the Royal Navy ship HMS *Otranto*, part of a convoy of food and troop ships. A Royal Navy reservist, he had been drafted into the navy at the outbreak of war. When he returned to England in June 1918 for seven days leave after two years away he was apparently in the best of health. Returning to his ship, he sailed again on 7 July, writing home that he had a touch of 'flu, but six days later he died of acute pneumonia, leaving a widow, two children and widowed invalided mother to share their grief. The same edition of the *Grays and Tilbury Gazette*, which carried the news of the ending of hostilities, also reported the death the previous month of two more Upminster men, Arthur Gray, who had died at the end of August, and Bert Burgess of the Sherwood Foresters, whose brother Charles had died in action the previous year.

It seems that the last Upminster soldier to lose his life during the war was Pte John Flack of the Essex Regiment whose death occurred on 5 November 1918, six days before the signing of the Armistice. Yet this was not the final serviceman's death. Two months later, on 8 January 1919 Lt Cyril Horncastle

Ernest Moore of Station Road, killed in action on 26 October 1918, was one of the last to die.

of Freshfields, Gaynes Park died of pneumonia in Cairo where he was attached to headquarters staff. The tragedy of his peace-time death was that he had served in the Middle East for over three and a half years since 1915 seeing and surviving 'much arduous service' and had never been home on leave. Although an Upminster resident he was a former student of Lindisfarne College, Westcliff and plans had been made 'for him to go up to Cambridge in April next'. Like so many young men of his 'lost' generation, these plans were not to be.

Only slowly did parish life return to some kind of normality, as over a long period soldiers were progressively demobilised and returned to civilian life. Others were released from their enforced captivity as prisoners of war: in January 1919 for instance, the release of three local men, Lance-Cpl. T. Williams, Pte. W. Gorden and Driver H. Nice, was reported. Belatedly, in late February, came the notification of the award of a Military Medal for Pte. W. Mansfield of the 26th Royal Fusiliers. By March 1919 only two cases remained at St Laurence Auxiliary Military Hospital and it was felt that the work of the unit, which had 'attended upwards of 300 men sent to them from Colchester, Warley and elsewhere' could now draw to a close. The final phase of its activities was 'a social gathering of an informal character… which evoked much gratitude from the patients'. On the 15 March the *Grays and Tilbury Gazette* reported a presentation made in recognition of work as assistant commander of the hospital by Miss Sophia C. Reilly, daughter of Charles Reilly of High House.

The parish celebrated peace with a number of thanksgiving services but the parading of captured German guns in February 1919 was a more public expression of the victory celebrations. At the start of December 1918 the parish council proposed a permanent memorial to the war dead, with a public meeting arranged as a first step. Discussions began in earnest in February 1919 but there was no agreement about the form of the memorial. Should it be a clock tower? Or perhaps a cross? Should the names of those who served in the war be listed or only those who fell? Should it cover only the armed services or include merchant naval men as well? What was in no doubt was that public subscriptions would be needed to meet the costs but there was no great enthusiasm to dig deep for this. By 31 March only £31 had been raised and the headline ran 'Is the war memorial in jeopardy?' A long debate at the annual parish meeting probably stirred more consciences but the fund crept up only slowly, reaching £100 by late May, whereas the estimated cost of a clock tower was in the range £400 to £850. Things were obviously not going well, for a new committee was elected.

While Upminster was still considering what to do, other nearby parishes were already unveiling their memorials or other tributes. On 11 December adjoining Cranham celebrated the completion of a stained glass window erected by public subscription. The following week, a full year after the question of a memorial was first raised, Upminster declared the result of its referendum. It seems that the clock tower proposal had fallen by the wayside, no doubt on cost grounds, and parishioners were asked to choose between a memorial hall or a monumental memorial. On 20 December 1919, it was reported that votes had split evenly between the two options: as there were insufficient funds for the hall, the monument finally won the day. The rector offered a site taken in from the churchyard in Corbets Tey Road and applied to the Diocese for the necessary faculty to carry out the works. Yet it was almost a further eight months before work was about to start. The cost was estimated at £610 but only £360 had been raised since the fund had started in December 1918. Moreover, the prominent local resident and architect Charles Reilly publicly savaged the Celtic cross design, which he felt was 'unworthy of the village'.

Despite the delay over the parish monument, a tribute to the dead was in evidence when a 'roll of honour' was exhibited at St Laurence church in August 1919, listing the names of forty-three war-dead with local connections. By June the following year the church was displaying a 'substantially framed roll of honour in perpetual memory of those men resident in or closely associated with the parish'; this listed fifty-eight names, not all of which were on the first list. On the last Sunday in September 1920 Upminster gained its first permanent memorial to those who fell, with the unveiling by Mr Henry Joslin, JP DL of Gaynes, of a brass commemorative plaque, naming thirteen members of that church. Wearing his uniform as deputy lieutenant of the county, Joslin spoke of 'the brave men who had poured out their life blood to save them from a mighty and unscrupulous foe'.

Yet it was to be seven months before the parish memorial on Corbets Tey Road was unveiled – continued lack of finance may well have been the delaying factor. The public ceremony was finally held before a large crowd on Sunday 8 May 1921 with Brigadier-General C.H. de Rougemont, DSO MVO, performing the official duties, 'removing the Union Jack which enshrouded' the memorial and making a valedictory speech. Those present would have formally witnessed for the first time memorial, designed by Mr C. Harrap, with 'a cross with Celtic ornamentation… rising from the massive Portland Stone cenotaph base', standing on three York stone steps; inscribed on the base were to be seen the names of sixty-six men with Upminster connections. The deliberations of the organising committee headed by Mr J.W. Gunnell in drawing up the final list and arranging the inscription of these names have not been preserved. Yet if they had intended the memorial to be a worthy commemoration of the parish's losses, then surely in the long time from conception to completion they could have taken more care in ensuring that the names of the fallen were accurately recorded, avoiding the several errors which somehow crept in.

Upminster's war memorial, unveiled on Sunday 8 May 1921.

4

HOMES FIT FOR HEROES

UPMINSTER IN THE 1920S

DURING THE WAR years in many areas house building activities came to a complete stop for the very good reasons that not only were building materials in short supply or unobtainable – the war effort took precedence – but also from 1915 onwards most eligible workers had joined the forces or had been switched to emergency work.

But things were a little different in Upminster, at least at first, as Griggs & Co. managed to continue with the work already underway and planned. In August 1914, when war began Ashburnham Gardens, Howard Road, Garbutt Road and Courtenay Gardens had just been finished. The following year saw the company submit plans for eight houses in Champion Road (now Nos. 9-23), two houses each in Hall Lane and Deyncourt Gardens, and a house in Engayne Gardens. The houses in Champion Road, for instance, were occupied in the summer of 1916 and there is evidence that houses were still being offered for sale in January 1917; certainly during 1916 and 1917 the company were active in discussions and agreements with the local council about their future building plans. In all probability, despite the effects of the hostilities, Griggs continued at least a limited level of building throughout the war.

Following the armistice, housing became an important national issue as Lloyd George and the National Liberal coalition swept to power on an election slogan of 'Homes fit for heroes'. The incoming government passed legislation to encourage building, both by private and council sectors, offering the so-called Addison Subsidy under which developers received a grant of £50 for houses with a maximum selling price of £550. The Romford Rural District Council considered where they could best develop in their locality and for a time some development in Upminster looked possible. In February 1921 one member of the parish council, Mr J.W. Gunnell, pressed the council to recognise the 'dire necessity for men's cottages in Upminster at a rental which would be within a working man's pocket' but it seems that his voice was outweighed by local objections, the most vociferous of which came from 'the

Champion Road, Upminster 5

The development of Champion Road, started by Dowsing & Davis around 1902, was completed after 1915 by Griggs & Co.

people over the bridge' – the inhabitants of the garden suburb. It was claimed in the *Grays and Tilbury Gazette* that their snobbery was accompanied by the 'iron-bound monopoly that rigidly shuts out any building contractor desirous of coming into the parish, and especially so if he proposes to erect houses to let and not to sell'. This perhaps explains why the following month, Upminster Parish Council wrote to the district council urging the abandonment of 'plans for the purchase of land and erection of dwellings'. Evidently these wishes were granted, for Romford Rural District Council's plans to build twenty-two council houses in Upminster failed to gain approval from the Minister of Health in October 1921.

The private development of the garden suburb was again in full swing soon after the ending of hostilities, and by March 1920 the Medical Officer for Health noted in his annual report plans to build fifty-two houses. The death at his Ilford home in August 1920 of Sir Peter Griggs (he had been knighted in 1916 for his war work, prior to being elected Member of Parliament for Ilford in 1918) marked the end of a short but important era of Upminster's history. After a service at Ilford Congregational Church, led by Griggs' long-standing friend and minister Rev. Charles Vine, well over 1,000 people joined the funeral procession accompanying his coffin to its final resting place in the Ilford Council Cemetery. In his address the Rev. Vine referred to Sir Peter as someone who had 'sound judgment, a strong will, and a wide experience of men and things', one whose 'religion was more in conduct than creed', someone who 'worked untiringly with a patience and thoroughness that were admired by all who knew him'. Although it could be said that Griggs' memorial in Upminster is the original Edwardian garden suburb, a more direct testimony was unveiled in the Congregational Church which he helped to establish in Station Road: the stained glass window at the back of the church inscribed 'Education, Religion, Industry, Benevolence', qualities which capture the essence of this Victorian self-made man.

Griggs' demise may have been a sad loss, but the company that bore his name continued, at least for a while, with William Garbutt Key now as the dominant force. The company's further development of the garden suburb was on the land bought from the Upminster Hall estate by Griggs in 1908 and added to in 1912 but as yet undeveloped. By February 1921, about the same time as the debate about building council houses was taking place, Key was already able to state that 'he had personally erected more houses during the last year than any individual builder in the east end of London'. But despite the company's original plans to develop 700 acres, the undeveloped land bank that they already held obviously ruled out further expansion. When the remainder of the Upminster Hall Estate, a further 478 acres and the Hall itself, were offered for sale at auction in January 1921 there was 'very little business' and no buyer could be found for the land or for the lordship of the manor, which was withdrawn at £350.

In March 1921 Griggs & Co. planned to extend building on the Upminster Hall estate to include Ingrebourne Gardens from Hall Lane to the Cranham boundary, Claremont Gardens between Deyncourt an Ingrebourne Gardens, and continuing on the north side (later to become Holden Way), and also a part of Grosvenor Gardens, southwards from Ingrebourne Gardens. The Romford District Council Building Committee was not impressed however, initially disapproving the plans and asking to interview the company. It was, however, to be well over ten years before the proposed development of this part of the estate was finally completed. By April 1921 Griggs and Co. announced that they already had twelve houses ready for occupation and were prepared to build and sell others for £850 freehold. In the following year it was reported that Upminster garden suburb was being 'greatly developed' and consisted of 'numerous' houses.

In March 1923 the five principal shareholders of W.P. Griggs & Co., including Sir Peter's widow, Lady Georgina Griggs, and W.G. Key, decided to put the company into voluntary liquidation and to dispose of the outstanding assets,

The Estate Office in Station Road of Upminster Estates Ltd, the successors to W.P. Griggs and Co.

which included undeveloped land and freehold houses on seven parcels of land in Hall Lane, Deyncourt, Ingrebourne, Claremont and Ashburnham gardens. The purchasers were Key himself, who bought three-eights, and another director of long-standing, the former east Somerset MP John William Howard Thompson, Griggs' solicitor, who acquired the principal holding of five-eights. Two years later these owners in turn sold their personal holding for £39,574 to Upminster Estates Ltd., of which they were also directors.

Other land from the Upminster Hall estate was put to different uses. On 28 July 1926 those attending a public meeting at the Bell Hotel decided to set up a limited company to establish a golf club for Upminster by acquiring the necessary land, either by purchase or by lease. The Directors appointed were soon able to acquire options to buy 77 acres and lease a further ten, all east of the Ingrebourne River and mostly west of Hall Lane. But by June 1927 just 25 applications had been received for the 800 available shares whose sale proceeds would part-fund the acquisition. Only a substantial purchase of shares by W.G. Key enabled the directors to proceed with the project, after which the company was incorporated on 2 July 1927. Golf was first played on 26 May 1928 on nine holes of the course designed by H.A.Colt, a golf architect, with work overseen by F.C. Plumbridge, the first club professional. Land which until a few months earlier had been 'barren and somewhat uninteresting... parts of which were always waterlogged' had been transformed

Upminster Hall was converted to provide a clubhouse for the newly formed Upminster Golf Club.

into tees and greens in 'first-class order' and fairways which 'presented a most attractive performance'. Upminster Hall had been converted into a 'commodious and inviting clubhouse' for which 'every comfort' had been 'catered for in its splendid furnishing'. Initially leased from the South Essex Brick and Tile Co., the freehold of the Hall was finally bought by the golf club in 1935. Further land had been added to the course in 1929, with additions in 1937, making a 5,693 yard par-70 course. The lordship of the manor was acquired from Upminster Estates by Essex County Council in 1938.

Other early post-war developments by Griggs & Co. were to the south of the railway and west of Station Road. On the Branfill Park Estate, after the completion of Champion Road, development continued westwards towards the boundary with Hornchurch. Highview Gardens was progressively built on a curving route behind Upminster Windmill down the slopes of the Ingrebourne valley from Champion Road to join with St Mary's Lane. Further west Cranborne Gardens was developed between Highview Gardens and the main road. Both were completed in 1924 and the roads formally taken over by the district council in February 1925.

W.P. Griggs & Co. had bought the manor and 65 acres estate of New Place to the south of Cranham Road from Capt. S.C. Umfreville of Baschurch, Salop, for £10,000 in September 1909. Stretching from behind the Bell Inn in the village centre, as far as the eastern parish boundary, the New Place estate consisted

Cranham Road, now St Mary's Lane, was often known as Clockhouse Lane, after the New Place Clockhouse.

'principally of park-like meadows'. From the west lawn a shrubbery led to a gateway opposite St Laurence church, allowing the occupiers a secluded stroll to the pew they maintained at their place of worship. Built in 1775, New Place, the last of Sir James Esdaile's buildings, was a large red brick house featuring twelve bedrooms. The western wing housed an impressive 35ft by 25ft drawing room or saloon, designed by the keen dancer Esdaile as a perfect venue for balls; the mantel was once noted for a portrait of him in a court dress and for its several fine mirrors. An eastern wing, which was almost wholly rebuilt in 1867 by the occupant Capt. Pelly, RN, housed the servants' quarters. The whole site was adorned by an elegant cedar tree, a typical landmark of Esdaile's development. But it was the stables and other buildings facing Cranham Road, which seem to have formed the greatest attachment for the people of Upminster. The clock which still graces them, dating from 1770 or earlier and originally from the top of the admiralty superintendent's house at Woolwich Arsenal, was the 'only public time-keeper in the neighbourhood', and 'one of Upminster's institutions'. This feature led to the whole property being referred to as 'The Clockhouse', rather than New Place.

Griggs' purchase of New Place had been on the understanding that no building would go ahead during the lifetime of the sitting tenant, John Wilson, the Scottish-born former chief engineer of the Great Eastern Railway. With the death in November 1922 of the seventy-six-year-old Wilson, the future of the estate became an important issue, as it was ideally placed for development. As early as 1915 the Clockhouse had been identified as a suitable location for the parish council's offices and by the end of October 1923 there was speculation that the parish council was considering the purchase of the site from Upminster Estates Ltd., who were asking £1,500 for a 60ft frontage on the newly-named St Mary's Lane, or £1,600 for an 80ft frontage, including the gardens at the rear.

The Clockhouse was preserved by Upminster Parish Council as the parish clerk's office, as well as providing facilities for the parish fire engine and ambulance.

The parish council decided to seek the views of the parishioners on whether to proceed and put forward a number of options for consideration: to buy Clockhouse and land for municipal offices; to buy Clockhouse, New Place and all adjoining land; or to provide accommodation for the parish clerk's office. The voting showed that although there was strong opposition to buying the complete site, there was strong support for premises for a clerk's office, and a bare majority (153/151) for the purchase of Clockhouse and adjacent land. Controversially perhaps, the parish council decided to go forward with the purchase of Clockhouse and land, for which they sought a loan of £2,000 from the Public Works Loan Office. Following the necessary support from Essex County Council in March 1924, a public enquiry was called by the Ministry of Health to consider the proposed loan application. This went ahead on Wednesday 7 May at the Commemoration Hall before Mr M.K. North, MICE, the government appointed inspector. Mr Albert Briebach, clerk to the council, put forward the parish's case: namely that the rapidly-expanding parish needed a better base from which to run its business than a front parlour in the clerk's house in Gaynes Road, which had been the centre of operations for fourteen years! Moreover, the parish fire apparatus was currently stored in a temporary wooden shed (at Talbot's Garage). With new houses going up at the rate of forty to forty-five each half-year, the situation demanded a permanent home for the council. The council had the chance to buy the Clockhouse for £1,140 and promised to spend £670 on essential repairs, using labour provided by the vendors Upminster Estates. But a few councillors and some ratepayers opposed the scheme, preferring instead only the purchase of offices for the clerk.

In June 1924 came a bombshell: the remaining part of New Place had been disposed of to a timber merchant for probable use as a timber yard with rumours of the possible erection of a sawmill. The parish was outraged! A well-attended parish meeting at the British School denounced the 'scandalous affair' and 'abomination'. It seemed, however, that the new owner, Frank Mayhew of Highgate, realised the storm he had caused and 'a reliable source' suggested that he would be prepared to offer the site back to the parish, although an inflated price of £2,750 was suggested. Meanwhile, by the end of August 1924 the main part of the New Place estate had been laid out for building and was being offered for building development at £10 per foot frontage; by now Esdaile's former mansion of New Place itself had almost certainly been demolished.

Within the parish council the debate raged on, with a few councillors fighting a sniping rearguard action to delay the possible purchase of Clockhouse, the agreement for which was literally waiting to be signed. To the surprise of many residents, in November 1924 the parish council's Chairman Mr G.C. Cardnell decided to call another parish meeting to gain support for the council's action once and for all, because he said that he had 'been assailed on so many occasions' by suggestions that the ballot of a year before had been confusing. The resulting parish meeting was notable for a 'heated exchange' of views between the chairman and his fiercest detractor, Mr Turner, but the proposal to buy Clockhouse was 'carried by a large majority and to loud applause', fully justifying Cardnell's decision. Now all the opposition had been silenced by the vote and this final hurdle had been surpassed, the sale could go ahead. By Christmas Eve 1924 discussions with the Public Works Loan Board were well advanced and the specifications for alteration and fitting had been drawn up. Once the loan was received early in the new year, the sale of Clockhouse from Upminster Estates to Frank Mayhew for £1,130 and the immediate resale to the parish council finally went ahead on 22 January 1925. At last Clockhouse had been saved for use as a public building.

As well as serving as the home for the parish clerk and council the Clockhouse was put to other local uses. Upminster had formed its own volunteer fire brigade in 1909 but with only a hand-truck at its disposal it was ill-equipped to deal with anything but the smallest fires. Major incidents required the parish to call on the services of the Hornchurch brigade, an inevitable source of friction, particularly over costs. After several disputes and mounting bad feeling, the parish's volunteer force was reformed in 1925 under the captaincy of an experienced retired fire officer, Mr John Bridger. A motorised fire engine was acquired in 1927, garaged in the newly acquired Clockhouse, which also served as an ambulance garage.

While the discussions about Clockhouse were continuing, building work on the New Place estate got going rapidly. In 1911, two years after Griggs & Co.'s acquisition of the estate, the question of its development had been first raised: at that time the Rural District Council's surveyor had recommended no drainage agreement should be sealed 'until plans have been approved and building has been commenced'. In May 1917 the company formally advised the council of its intention to start laying out the estate for building and were asked to submit building notices and plans, and the drainage agreement was finalised.

From its northern boundary along Cranham Road, the New Place estate as between 1,000 and 1,700ft deep, its boundaries now marked by Sunnyside Gardens on the western and southern sides and by Argyle Gardens to the east, where the parish boundary with Cranham followed the rear line of the back of the gardens on the eastern side. These roads formed the earliest part of the estate's development, working southwards from Cranham Road. The building of Argyle Gardens had already started by the summer of 1921, probably earlier, and progressively extended over the next few years: by the autumn of 1922 plans for Nos. 33-39 and 36-42 had been approved. By February 1925 the district council had taken over the road some 320ft southwards of the by now named St Mary's Lane. Houses up to No. 115 were occupied by the summer of 1926, with the even numbers (up to No. 90) complete by the next year, by which time Sunnyside Gardens had also been built. In 1927 as work on Sunnyside and Argyle Gardens drew to a close, the development of Cedar, Tudor and New Place Gardens began. Building started in Tudor Gardens, running south from St Mary's Lane parallel to Sunnyside, but more progress was made with Derham Gardens, named after Upminster's most famous rector, completed in the spring or summer of 1928 and occupied by the autumn of that year.

Until the sale of the Clockhouse gardens to the parish council was concluded, no building took place in the square which bordered these grounds, and only the south side of Cedar (even numbers) and the east side of New Place (odd numbers) were built at first. But after the sale in March 1929 to the parish council of the gardens adjoining Clockhouse, the roads surrounding the council-owned site were developed. By the mid-1920s the bungalow had emerged as a popular form of suburban housing. The middle classes of India's Raj had lived in long low detached single storey dwellings, and the name bungalow – from the word 'Bangla', the area known as Bengal or Bangladesh – came to describe this housing type. It was perhaps inevitable that Upminster's growth should include this form of housing and this phase of the New Place Estate provided Upminster's first substantial bungaloid development. The completion of the north (odd numbers) side of Cedar Gardens early in 1931 brought to a close the building of this estate which added over 400 houses and bungalows to Upminster's housing stock.

Tudor Gardens and other roads on the New Place Estate included bungalows – an increasingly popular housing feature at this time.

More housing fronted St Mary's Lane from Argyle Gardens almost to Tudor Gardens but the prime sites from here to the Bell Corner were given over to commercial development. At the end of July 1922 the *Grays & Tilbury Gazette* was still able to note 'that the south side of Cranham Road just now presents a scene of tress and meadows' but went on to warn that 'sites have been taken for a garage and a chemist's shop etc.' The garage was on a key corner site, at the junction of Sunnyside Gardens, which now houses a Shell petrol station. The Upminster Garage developed on the site offered a full range of motoring services from petrol to car repairs and car hire and driving instruction, as well as arranging insurance.

The 1920s saw a boom in Britain's fledgling cinema industry, particularly after the 'talkies' were introduced in 1927. Massive 'picture palaces' seating thousands rapidly sprang up all around London and its developing suburbs. Upminster was no exception and the prestige site at the junction of St Mary's Lane and Tudor Gardens – now Somerfield's Supermarket – became the 1,100 seat Capitol 'super-cinema', rapidly developed during 1929 to the design of Mr James Hatfield at a cost of £25,000. The doors first opened to the public on Thursday 10 October 1929, when a long queue 'from all parts of the district, including Grays and Dagenham' awaited the opening by Mr J.W. Gunnell, chairman of Upminster Parish Council. The audience were in for a surprise, for 'the opening ceremony was performed by a talkie film specially prepared for

The Capitol Cinema opened in St Mary's Lane on 10 October 1929.

the occasion', Mr Gunnell appearing on screen. The first programme offered one talkie – Richard Barthemess in *Parasites* – and a supporting silent film – Monty Banks in *Adam's Apple* ('A super silent comedy') – and Mr W.T. Chapman playing the 'John Compton Super-British Organ' as an added attraction. Admission prices ranged from 8*d* to 2*s* 4*d* with continuous performances from 2pm to 10.30pm. There were two programmes weekly, from Thursday to Saturday (no Sunday performances for many years) and Monday to Wednesday. Part of Mr D.J. James' cinema circuit, along with the Mayfair at Beacontree Heath, Dagenham (opened 1933) and the Towers at Hornchurch, built 1935, the Capitol was renamed the Odeon in 1948, before becoming the Gaumont two years later. It closed as a cinema on 5 July 1961 and was redeveloped and operated as a Top Rank bingo club before its demolition in 1974.

Other changes throughout the 1920s provided Upminster with increasing links to its neighbours. From 20 June 1921 Messrs Harding & Rowley, two ex-servicemen, offered an independent 'pirate' bus service providing eight to ten journeys daily between their home town of Romford and Upminster. On 7 September the same year came the 'official' service, when Upminster was linked to the London General Omnibus Company's network, with a double-decker motorbus service running fifteen times a day to Stratford, via Hornchurch (the 86 bus route). In April 1929 Upminster's new much-enlarged telephone exchange, to replace the original small facility on the upper floor of Green's

Store on the corner of Howard Road, opened in a new building on St Mary's Lane, near the junction with Sunnyside Gardens. The first major road links came with the building of the London-Southend Arterial Road (now the A127) through the northern half of the parish, cutting across Hall Lane. In January 1922 one thousand men were reported to be at work on the Hornchurch to Upminster section, although it was over three years before HRH Prince Henry performed the formal opening on 25 March 1925. By the end of the decade came the news that main route would pass the southern end of the parish (the A13). These developments all enhanced Upminster's value as a popular location for building.

Towards the end of the 1920s came another step that preserved Upminster's character – the purchase of the 18 acre glebelands running south from the church, bordering Corbets Tey Road. After long discussions in August 1929 the parish council reached agreement with the Rector Hyla Henry Holden to buy this important site for the enjoyment of the people of the parish. A purchase price of £5,500 was agreed, a loan of £5,375 was approved by the Ministry of Health and the sale was completed at the end of November 1929. The glebeland was already a recognised location for recreation, for in early 1920 the part of it known as Rectory Meadow had become the wicket and ground for Upminster Cricket Club, after the former ground in Hall Lane had been rendered unfit for use through being used as horse-lines for the Bucks

An Upminster Cricket Club team from the 1920s.
Back row: H. Payne (umpire); J. Jackson; C. Halliday; G. W. Tyler; A. Guest; W. Jackson; J. Burrell; J. Pratt (scorer).
Front row: H. Jones; H. Gillman; G. G. Gross; W. Aldous; Rev H. R. Holden.

Yeomanry during the war. The club's pavilion, an old railway carriage, survived the move from the Hall Lane location but the club had to raise a loan of £20 to buy iron hurdles from the Hornchurch CC to fence off the wicket after matches, in order to keep cattle from grazing on it! The pavilion lasted until mid-1933 when one Saturday night it caught fire and was completely gutted. The Hornchurch UDC, who became the owners of the ground the following year upon the demise of the parish council, were sympathetic to the club's plight and, in consideration for an increased rent, agreed to provide a permanent pavilion which was ready for use by the start of the summer 1935 season. Another tenant of the Recreation Ground, as it became known, was the Upminster Wanderers Football Club, founded in 1921, who played on the front of the ground adjoining Corbets Tey Road, opposite what later became the location of the Woolworths store. The club remained there until their relocation in 1953 to the new stadium in Bridge Avenue. Already retitled 'Upminster Football Club', on the move to the new site they changed their name to Hornchurch and Upminster Football Club.

So at the end of the 1920s Upminster had witnessed significant changes, which by far dwarfed the pre-First World War developments. Between 1921 and 1931 the number of families in the parish increased by nearly two-thirds from 533 to 870, while the population rose in proportion from 3,559 to 5,732. The modernisation of the Essex beauty spot had reached an irreversible stage and, as the next chapter shows, Upminster was poised on the threshold of the next major steps – the transformation of the southern part of the parish.

GREAT GAYNES . . . BUT ALSO MANY LOSSES

UPMINSTER IN THE 1930S

IT WAS THE death on 2 November 1927 of Henry Joslin, DL JP, owner and lord of the manor of Gaynes, that was to prove the key that opened the door to the development of southern Upminster. As an obituary said, Joslin was a 'typical specimen of a "fine English gentleman"... aristocratic in bearing... and courteous to a degree' – indeed all the qualities to be expected in a deputy lieutenant of the county. Born in 1839, the son of Henry Joslin of Hoppey Hall, and Priscilla, widow of George Gooding, in 1865 he had married Rebecca Mary, widow of the Rev. George Clayton of Gaynes Park. Mrs Clayton had inherited Gaynes for life in 1862 on the death of her husband, a noted Congregational minister, like his father and two brothers. Possibly her marriage to Joslin was rooted more in business sense than romance for she was some twenty-five years older than her second husband; not surprisingly the couple had no children. (In contrast she had been junior to her first husband by a similar degree.)

Mrs Joslin died on Christmas Eve 1873 after a long illness, aged fifty-nine; her husband, just thirty-four, never remarried. Under the terms of the Rev. Clayton's will the Gaynes estate had to be sold on her death and in June 1874 Hubert Atkin Gilliat Esq became the owner, adding the adjoining 54 acre Londons estate soon afterwards. Gilliat's attempts to set up a large-scale dairy farm were unsuccessful and in 1877 he sold the combined holding of Gaynes and Londons to Henry Joslin.

During Sir James Esdaile's ownership in the late eighteenth century, the Gaynes estate had extended to some 750 acres, but it was broken up in 1820 when 540 acres were sold. After Joslin bought Gaynes he almost restored the estate to its former glories, adding the 98 acre Hoppey Hall Farm in 1887, and Hunts Farm of 130 acres two years later; at the time of Joslin's death in 1927 Gaynes comprised some 404 acres. Gaynes mansion itself was of no great antiquity, dating only to 1846 when it was rebuilt by Clayton on the site of the former house. In Wilson's view it had 'some points of architectural

Henry Joslin DL (1839–1927) of Gaynes Park.

interest' notably the entrance 'of bold proportions... surmounted by a corbelled window' and large mullioned stained-glass windows on the western side, giving 'light to the staircase and central hall'. In all there were on the ground floor a drawing and dining rooms, library and 'offices', with upstairs some seven bedrooms and two servants' bedrooms, a dressing room and bathroom. The grounds remained largely as Esdaile had conceived them with 'venerable elms of large dimensions' and many 'flourishing' and 'beautiful' wych-elms. Nearby was a 'detached residence or dower house', known as Little Gaynes, built in a similar but much smaller scale to the main house. Great Gaynes, or Gaynes Park as it was often styled, lay to the south of Little Gaynes Lane and was reached by a drive guarded at each end by a lodge. Opposite the entrance to the drive at the eastern end at Gaynes Cross was the East Lodge (still surviving as 201 Corbets Tey Road). At the western end of the drive on Little Gaynes Lane stood West Lodge, a small thatched cottage, the home of Joslin's coachman. Destroyed by fire in 1908, it was rebuilt in the same style.

In April 1928, five months after Henry Joslin's death, came the first attempt to dispose of the Gaynes estate as a single entity of some 404 acres. The agent's sale catalogue drew attention to the benefits of the area and the estate, describing Upminster as a location where 'important building development is taking place and which is now regarded as one of the most progressive Essex suburbs'. The Gaynes estate was said to include 'three miles of frontage to main and district roads and all public services' and was claimed to be 'ripe for development... as a building estate for houses of medium size'. But the sale was unsuccessful and a change of tack was called for before the holding was marketed fifteen months later in July 1929. Gaynes had been repackaged into seventeen lots, six of which were two or less acres, comprising the houses and gardens of Hunts Farm, Hoppey Hall, Londons, Tadlows and three and four cottages adjacent. The largest lot was 82 acres surrounding Hoppey Hall, with Hunts and Tadlows farms offered as 81 acre and 68 acre plots. Gaynes Park was split into three lots, the largest, of 61 acres, running south from

The manor house of Great Gaynes was of no great antiquity or architectural merit.

Gaynes mansion to the lake. A further attraction was that plans for the estate's development had been laid before the planning authorities at Romford. A draft scheme provided that 'the density of houses shall not exceed 12 to the acre, that the road to Corbets Tey shall be widened to 50 foot with a 20 foot building line'. The developers were required to construct a new 60ft wide road running east-west across the whole development, now known as Gaynes Park Road to the west and Park Drive to the east, crossing Corbets Tey Road and continuing westwards until it joined Little Gaynes Lane. Clearly, no longer was Gaynes to be covered with 'houses of medium size', as the earlier catalogue had proposed, and the firm principles established in this development brief were fully in keeping with Griggs' original Edwardian garden suburb.

Although the auction of Gaynes Park in July 1929 attracted 'considerable interest' bidding was very slow, causing the auctioneer, Mr George Eve of Hoppey Hall, to remark 'surely you are not here out of curiosity?' Of the first thirteen lots offered for sale, there were only two sales: a 27 acre plot of 'building land' north of Harwood Hall Lane, sold to Mr Allen Ansell, a well-known developer, for £3,000, and Hoppey Hall, bought by a bidder acting on behalf of the tenant (and auctioneer) Eve for £2,500. Gaynes Park itself, and its sixteen surrounding acres south of Little Gaynes Lane, remained unsold but was bought immediately after the auction by H.A. Dowsett, JP, of Southend.

Large areas either failed to reach their reserve price or attract any bidding at all, but four smaller lots near Corbets Tey had a better fate and were disposed of. The unsold lots were afterwards sold by private treaty to development companies, the first plot sold in this way being the 9 acre plot described as 'Naboth's vineyard' and subsequently developed as Stewart Avenue and the shops fronting Corbets Tey Road on either side of it.

As was the normal pattern, the estate development companies who had bought the land planned and laid out the roads (with kerbstones) and provided main services – gas, water, sewage – marking out individual numbered plots or groups of plots for builders to start to erect houses on. On the Gaynes estate this approach extended to sales to approved builders who agreed to build only approved types of dwellings. Estate stipulations were imposed which set out the minimum floor area of the dwellings to be built, together with other 'restrictions' to ensure the best possible development within the prevailing demand. Rural tranquillity soon gave way to the sound of large, automatic trenching machines carving out deep trenches for the main sewers. The earliest building work was started on the lands south of Hoppey Hall, where the developers were the Gaynes Park Estates Ltd. of Westcliff-on-Sea who were obliged to lay out the principal route of Gaynes Park Road from Corbets Tey Road to its now-existing junction with Little Gaynes Lane.

The first houses on the Gaynes Park Estate were those fronting Corbets Tey Road, adjacent to The Approach, followed by South View Drive, Gaynes Park Road and Little Gaynes Lane. West of Corbets Tey Road and north of Gaynes Park Road the area was developed to become what are known as the 'tree roads': Elm and Beech Avenues sported the first houses in 1931, with Oak Avenue following around 1933, reaching Maple Avenue and Sycamore Drive the next year, and then Acacia Drive. Several builders were at work, including Donovan and Whitaker of Leigh-on-Sea, A. Wheeler and J. Clarke, both of Westcliff, and Mr A. Whistler. Prices in the early 1930s ranged from £765 for a three-bedroom semi-detached house in Oak Avenue built by Clarke to £875 for a Wheeler-built detached house in Gaynes Park Road, with detached 'semi-bungalows' (on two floors) in Little Gaynes Lane offered for £1,050.

A few years later in 1936 houses on the Gaynes Park Estate were advertised as 'good honest value' from £655 freehold which the purchasers could repay as rent. Keys of show houses could always be obtained (Sundays included) from the estate office on the corner of The Approach. 'No applicant for key', the advert ran, 'will be pressed to purchase'. By the late 1930s the estate was nearing completion, except for part of South View Drive and Cedar Avenue and the additional section north of Little Gaynes Lane that was to become Lime Avenue, Hornbeam Avenue, Alder Avenue and Aspen Grove. By 1939 roads and services had been laid but two bungalows only had been built in Hornbeam. This remaining section of the estate was only completed in the 1950s.

Park Drive was designed as a main thoroughfare across the Gaynes Park Estate.

To the east of Corbets Tey Road development went ahead at a similar speed on the former farmlands of Hunts, north and south of the other new thoroughfare Park Drive. To the north of Park Drive, where Southend-on-Sea Estates Ltd. were the developers of what was to become the Springfield Estate, building progressed away from Corbets Tey Road, in this case working eastwards with the first houses appearing in Meadow Way in 1932. This estate was noted for its considerable flair, particularly those houses built in Meadow Way, Fairfield Drive and Springfield Gardens by Mr H.W. Wire of Hornchurch who designed and built his own houses and bungalows, rather than work from pattern books as did many builders. Rushmore Avenue had been reached by 1935 and Roxburgh Avenue two years later. Another main builder on the Springfield Estate was Mr A. Kind of Westcliff, who operated from 114 Springfield Gardens, building houses in Leasway, and some in Springfield Gardens and Meadow Way. By the outbreak of war in 1939 this estate was substantially completed.

On the south side of Park Drive an early start was made on land acquired for development by A.E. (Alfred) Palmer of Billericay. Work began at the southern boundary where Cranston Park Avenue began to take shape in 1932, progressively extending eastwards, while Melstock Avenue progressed southwards from the newly established Park Drive to join it. Brackendale Gardens also worked its way southwards from 1933, as did Coniston Avenue, both being completed by 1936, by which time Cranston Park Avenue was near completion.

Gaynes Senior School in Brackendale Gardens started building in July 1936, with the first intake of pupils joining the school that September. However, the far eastern end of Park Drive remained unfinished when war began in 1939 and the partly-completed buildings served the local children as an impromptu adventure playground.

Gaynes house itself had probably been demolished early in October 1930 so that the London-based developers Great Gaynes Estates Ltd. could prepare the surrounding grounds for housing plots. As befitted its former glory, the 16 acre lawn and parkland site was developed in more individual style than elsewhere on the Gaynes Park Estate. Not surprisingly, the main detached houses on this site and on Tawny Avenue were tagged by names rather than numbers. In February 1935 for instance MacGregor invited would-be purchasers to 'Select your own plot on Parkland Avenue and have a house built to your own specification'. This style of development was not without its problems as the estates further and more remote from the station proved to be less popular and development proceeded more slowly, to be interrupted by the onset of war.

The Foxhall Estate on the east side of Corbets Tey Road was not part of the Gaynes estate as it had been in private ownership. The house of Foxhall itself was originally built in 1718 and had been known at various times as Foxhunters Hall or Vauxhall. According to Wilson it had a 'well-designed centre and wings; the southern forming an elegant dining room'. Other features were a staircase with a 'finely-carved rail . . . and hung with tapestry', a walled garden and a fish-pond. By 1938 this area had also been laid out with roads – now Freshfields Avenue, Hall Park Road and Fox Hall Road – by the developers Gaynes Park Estates Ltd. Only a few dwellings, principally bungalows in Freshfields Avenue and Hall Park Road, had been built and occupied by the outbreak of war in 1939.

To the north of Hoppey Hall, from 1933 the 9 acre field known as the Hoppit or Naboth's Vineyard became the location of the single road development of Stewart Avenue and shops on Corbets Tey Road. This had no links to other roads on the Gaynes Park development, except for the footpath which formerly crossed the site, preserved as a less direct right of way. Stewart Avenue's junction with Corbets Tey Road was flanked by newly erected shops. By 1934 Hoppey Hall's 'old world garden with a fine cedar tree, flower beds, partly-walled kitchen garden . . . full-sized tennis-court' and its once rural aspect, were hemmed in on three sides by buildings. 'Doubtless one of the oldest houses in the parish', dating from the seventeenth century or earlier, it was a 'capacious square timber and plastered building with three fronts and square clustered chimneys'. Among Hoppey Hall's previous occupiers were J. Williams Benn, MP for St George's East and Wapping, grandfather of the Labour politician Anthony Wedgwood Benn. Benn rented the house from September 1891 and during the summer months he produced and acted in open-air dramatic productions on the lawn, with all the family and many local people marshalled into performing or making costumes or scenery. This local interlude ended when the Benns, beset by financial problems, moved on a few years later in June 1894.

Hoppey Hall, probably dating from the seventeenth century or earlier, formed part of the Gaynes Park Estate, auctioned after Henry Joslin's death.

George Eve, who had bought Hoppey Hall in 1929 at the Gaynes Park auction, instructed Messrs H.V. & G. Sorrell to dispose of the premises in October 1935 and asked the recently formed Hornchurch District Council whether they wished to buy it, but they decided that it was 'not desirous'. In February 1938 Eve announced that he would shortly be leaving the district and three months later in May 1938 Hoppey Hall was offered for sale by auction as a site suitable for shops and flats. The purchaser for £5,000 was Mr Alexander D. MacGregor, the local builder whose estate office was at 113 Corbets Tey Road. MacGregor stated that he had bought Hoppey Hall because he was 'interested in Upminster' and wished to develop the site 'in a manner worthy of Upminster'. He had 'no immediate plans for its development' and expected it to 'remain very little changed for a year or two'. Two years earlier there had been much speculation about the possible building of a 'super cinema' in Corbets Tey Road by Springfield Drive, with seating for some 2,500 and parking for 1,500, casting doubts over the future of the Capitol Cinema in St Mary's Lane. These plans came to nothing but during 1938 MacGregor had negotiations with a cinema circuit about developing Hoppey Hall for this purpose but these discussions broke down early in 1939 when the prospects of war seemed inevitable. Towards the end of January 1939 the fine old house was demolished. The magnificent cedar tree which had stood at the front of the site was felled by MacGregor two months later, just in advance of the arrival of officials from Hornchurch UDC bearing a Tree Preservation Order.

Hornchurch and Upminster News
24 March 1939

Many have been the repercussions following the felling of the famous Hoppey Hall cedar tree. Mr J.P. Mansell of Cranston Park Avenue has written the following sonnet:

> The cedar tree in Corbets Tey
> Is down and we who pass that way
> View with dismay the vacant space
> Which once was a shimmering green.
> That quiet shade, that lovely scene,
> Those rugged boughs of sturdy grace
> Whereon the thrush with cheerful glee
> Challenged the gale in ecstasy,
> All disappeared and in that place
> ...Who knows?
> No treacherous winds or heavy snows,
> No lighting cruel did thee disgrace;
> 'Twas modern progress sealed thy fate
> And we are left disconsolate.

The war intervened. By the time that the Hoppey Hall site was again marketed in May 1946 it was said to be 'suitable for the erection of a cinema, shops and flats'. In October 1946 the County of London Electricity Company bought a small part of the site for £560 for the erection of an election sub-station. Part of the rest was sold to the Post Office in 1952, leading to the later building of the sorting office, and five years later, when Hornchurch UDC were seeking sites for car parks, the remaining half was sold to them for this purpose.

In June 1935, High House, opposite the churchyard, was put on the market by the son and daughter of the most recent owner Charles Reilly, a prominent London architect who had died in June 1928. Once the home of Upminster's most famous incumbent, Dr William Derham, in whose days of the late seventeenth century it was already old, the ancient house together with its famous cedar tree, almost 20ft in girth, was pulled down in September 1935 leading to considerable speculation about what uses the prestigious central site would be put. The purchasers were 'The Academy Electric Building Co. (1931)' of Manor Park, a company of which the three directors were each proprietors of successful businesses in High Street North, East Ham and Manor Park, who in recent years had combined to handle other development projects. The speculation ended in January 1936 when plans were submitted to and approved by Hornchurch UDC for a 'palatial block of flats' on two storeys, Byron Parade (claimed to be 'the finest residential flats for miles around') and the sixteen shops on a frontage of 380ft in Corbets Tey Road. Further ambitious plans for the rest of the four acre site laid before the Hornchurch Council in May 1936 had included a concert hall and a swimming pool, 100ft long by 40ft wide and catering for 1,000 bathers and 500 spectators, a café and a restaurant at a cost of £35,000. But in the event this grandiose venture fell through and instead some of the proposed site was sold for £1,000 to Essex County Council as an addition to the playing fields for the primary school in St Mary's Lane.

CORBETS TEY ROAD, UPMINSTER.

The shops in Byron Parade, pictured here around 1960, opened in the summer of 1936 on the site of the High House.

The first shops in Byron Parade were let in August 1936, with Craddocks 'stationers and fancy goods specialists of Romford and Westcliff-on-Sea' offering, at No. 6, a free gift of 'high grade stationery' to the first 500 customers spending not less than 1s, while at No. 2 Messrs L.S. Green, radio dealers

'well known in the district' opened their modern and spacious showroom...
lit by concealed lighting', selling all the latest radio sets – 'products of this
modern wonder of the world' – including those by 'Ekco, Pye, Ultra, G.E.C
and Mullard'. The Parade's shops which stood 20ft back from the kerb per-
mitted shoppers 'a free inspection of the windows of the premises without
any obstruction by passers-by, as is often experienced in other places where a
narrow pavement makes shopping a tedious business'.

Hunts farmhouse, which had been part of the Gaynes Park sale in 1929, was
again offered for sale by auction on 20 February 1936 as a 'freehold building
site possessing a frontage to Corbets Tey Road of about 294 feet... considered
ripe for the erection of shops'. Hunts was a tall, square ten-bedroom Georgian
farmhouse, built by Sir James Esdaile, standing on Corbets Tey Road at the
corner of what is now Springfield Gardens. The farmhouse and farmlands had
been added to the Gaynes Estate by Henry Joslin in 1890 and farmed by his
brother Walter who died in January 1923. Hunts was demolished around 1937
and shops and the attractive flats of Springfield Court were built to the rear.

The scale of construction of the estates accessible from Corbets Tey Road
was considerable, with eighteen builders active there during the peak years of
the mid-1930s. As the *Upminster Chronicle* noted in October 1935:

> In many parts of the district there is taking place a rapid and unostentatious
> development, both for residential and business purposes which is changing the
> face of what was once a quiet Essex backwater. Old buildings are being demol-
> ished, new houses and shops are being thrown up on a number of estates and
> other land is being earmarked for development.

Credit for Upminster's environment should also be given to the builders at
that time. Among them were carpenters and bricklayers who worked on site
in their own trade drawing a weekly wage and producing upwards of six
houses a year. As most houses were built 'on spec' the actual number they
built depended on how many they could sell. Consequently there was keen
competition between builders and some were more successful than others.
The particular design and location of properties was a factor, as was price,
with a difference of as little as £20 on an average cost of around £800 greatly
influencing prospective purchasers.

The 1930s also witnessed the latter stages of the Upminster Hall Estate, although
the peak activity for Upminster Estates Ltd. had now passed and the company
was running down as war approached. Claremont Gardens was completed by
1935, while the westwards extension of Waldegrave Gardens began in 1934 and
continued until the outbreak of war. The development of individual plots on
The Fairway had started by 1934, as had Holden Way, built northwards from
Ingrebourne Gardens. Further up Hall Lane Spenser Crescent was being offered

During the 1920s and '30s work continued on the Upminster Hall Estate eastwards towards the boundary with Cranham.

for sale by 1936, with Masefield Drive following in 1937. The 'freehold artistic houses and bungalows' on this Hall Lane Estate were being sold by Derrick Construction Ltd. from £750 in 1936 'all roads made, all charges paid'.

Upminster was particularly lucky that its development was in the hands of responsible land development companies and individuals of the calibre of A.E. Palmer. In contrast to many suburban areas, the development of southern Upminster was well planned and provided an appropriate continuation to the pleasant environment of Griggs' garden suburb. In nearby Laindon by contrast land companies had sold individual plots by auction from marquees to people attracted by the claimed virtues of home ownership in a rural setting with access to London. Subsequent development there was fragmented, unplanned and consequently of a disjointed nature and consisting of brick and timber buildings of various shapes and sizes, without the benefits of main drainage or services. The sites, which at the time of the summer auctions no doubt seemed dry, often turned into rutted muddy condition in winter, with unmade roads which became impassable quagmires.

Alfred Charles Salinger appears to have been among the most prolific of the builders. Established in Upminster in 1932, starting with Coniston Avenue on the Cranston Park Estate, Salinger moved on to three further estates, Gaynes Park, the Springfield Estate and in post-war years to the Foxhall Estate and the last section of Gaynes Park bounded by Little Gaynes Lane and Hacton Lane. In 1938 for instance on the Springfield Estate A. C. Salinger & Co. offered 'distinctive' houses and bungalows of 'varied designs to suit all purchasers'; all were architectur-

Alfred Charles Sallinger (1889-1974)

ally designed, with 'external and internal walls entirely of brick'.

Born in Bow in 1889 into a family which had long connections with the printing and publishing industry, Alfred Salinger left school at thirteen and, while waiting for a job in his father's firm to fall vacant, took a post as an office boy in Poultry in the City. A year or so later, whilst working in a printing office in East Ham where the family were living, young Salinger was 'rescued' from a job which seemed to offer little prospects by his Sunday school superintendent, a master joiner, who offered him an apprenticeship at half a crown a week. This training provided the foundations for his later career in the building trade. During the First World War, newly married, he volunteered for service using his carpentry skills as a sergeant instructor in the Royal Naval Air Service, working on the earliest wooden bi-planes. After the war ended he worked as a shop-fitter before branching out in business around 1930, in partnership with Mr George J. Bragg, a master builder of Clements Road, East Ham, trading as Bragg & Salinger. Salinger, his wife and daughter moved from East Ham to Upminster in January 1936 after the completion of the building of his own house at No. 15 Park Drive. After Bragg's death in November 1937 A.C. Salinger & Co. was formed, becoming a limited company in 1940.

Salinger became a highly respected local figure, serving as councillor on the Hornchurch Urban District Council from 1938-62, as a magistrate (1947-64) and Deputy Chairman within the Romford Division of the Petty Sessions. He was one of the founder members of the Rotary Club of Hornchurch in 1946 and also convened the meeting which launched the Hornchurch and District Chamber of Commerce in the same year. His strong interest in education resulted in his service locally as Chairman of Hornchurch Grammar School and St Mary's Lane ('The Bell School') and in the wider area as chairman of the Education Committee of the South East Division of Essex County Council. A keen sportsman, outside work his interests included cricket, which he played for many years, and football, in which he was a qualified referee, on the list of the major amateur leagues. He worked until he was eighty in 1969, after which the company was wound up, and he died in 1974 aged eighty-five.

One of Upminster's attractions, according to the main selling agents Gates & Son (as they then were), was that its title as 'an Essex beauty spot' was 'richly deserved'. Gates' publicity in the 1930s was clearly aimed at the middle classes, drawing readers' attention to the 'houses of pleasing design and artistic merit' that were being built. There were said to be a number of good private schools in the neighbourhood, of which the accessibility of Palmers School, Grays was mentioned, while among the 'indoor entertainments' described were whist drives, a dramatic club, and a Masonic lodge. The publicity advised intending residents to contact local firms whose adverts appeared with 'initial orders for household requirements . . . a few days before the proposed arrival to take up residence, so as to ensure delivery of all requirements promptly.' (Just try that today!)

So who were these families who populated the vastly expanded Essex garden suburb? In the main they came from parts of 'Essex in London' such as Ilford, Barking, East Ham, Upton Park and Forest Gate. Whereas many of the early migrants to Upminster had been attracted by the steam link to Fenchurch Street, some of these newer commuters were equally attracted by the electric District Line service which was extended from Barking to reach Upminster in September 1932 after two years' creation and the reconstruction of the existing LMS line, including the widening and enlargement of the station bridge. The opening of the new line was greeted calmly at Upminster, unlike at the new Dagenham Heathway station where 'remarkable scenes were witnessed' as over two thousand people booked in advance. There were only a handful on the pioneer train leaving Upminster at 5.08 am on Monday 12 September but 'further up the line there was more eagerness to patronise the new service'. In addition to the Fenchurch Street service Upminster now gained sixteen trains during the morning peak from 6.30 am to 9 am, with fifteen evening peak arrivals, as well as a new signal box and six new carriage sidings. A quarterly season ticket to London cost £3 13s 3d in 1936 – little more than it had thirty years before when the Edwardian suburb had begun.

By 1934 a station followed at Upminster Bridge, just across the boundary in Hornchurch, and this proved more convenient for some residents on the estate built near the western parish boundary. Brookdale Avenue and the first section of Bridge Avenue were developed south of St Mary's Lane after 1931 and a start was made on Boundary Road from 1937. This area however, on the site of the former Bridge House Farm, was immediate post-war period, with Bridge Avenue joining Acacia Drive to provide a road link to the Gaynes Park Estate to the south.

Another fruitful source of residents for the expanding Upminster came from the setting up of the massive Ford Motor Company factory on the Dagenham marshes from 1929 and which began production in 1931. Many management staff and other employees relocated with the company from their former centre near Manchester. Good relationships between the letting and selling agent and the Ford personnel manager ensured that Upminster became a chosen place of residence

Detached houses, such as this newly built one in Ingrebourne Gardens, proved attractive to Ford executives.

for many seeking better-quality houses to buy or rent within reasonable travelling distance.

Had the war not intervened, Upminster may have been less pleasant than it is today. By 1937 plans had been approved by the county and local authorities to allow the development for housing of the area eastwards from the Upminster-Cranham boundary, running from the rear of Argyle Gardens tight up to Cranham church and beyond. This development, on over 400 acres of the Cranham Hall Farm, part of the huge Benyon estate, would have included an eastwards extension of Park Drive and a main 5oft road southwards from St Mary's Lane, running through what is now Coopers' Company and Coborn School, joining the Ockendon Road just east of Corbets Tey Cemetery. Bought by Dowsett of Southend and others when the Benyon estate was auctioned in June 1937, many of the builders active in Upminster took up options for development. However, two events combined to stop the proposals going forward: the intervention of war in 1939, which put a virtual halt to building developments and the impact of the Green Belt Act of 1938 which fixed a girdle of permanent open countryside around London's urban sprawl, as a means of preventing further erosion of the countryside. This was reinforced in 1947 by the major overhaul of British planning laws which made the preservation of the Metropolitan Green Belt a major policy objective. In this way Upminster's eastwards spread was halted and the boundary with Cranham running south from St Mary's signifies the end of urban London and the start of rural Essex.

The lack of a population census in 1941 due to the war means that there can be no precise measure of Upminster's growth during the 1930s. Just as there had been a rise of between half and two-thirds in each of the previous three decades, what evidence there is suggests a similar or even greater expansion had taken place during the pre-war decade. By 1951 the population had reached 13,000, double the 1931 level; a population of over 9,000 'and rapidly increasing' was already being claimed by an estate agent in 1934, a population of 11,000 or so in 1941 was probable. There can be little doubt that the 1930s saw the most significant period of growth in Upminster's history.

6

HITLER v. UPMINSTER

THE SECOND WORLD WAR

As THE 1930s drew to a close the aggressive stance of Hitler's Nazi Germany against its neighbours and its piecemeal invasion led to the increasing likelihood that war would result. With memories of the First World War still fresh in the minds of the middle-aged, it was the fear of war with all its consequences which fostered a reluctance to accept its inevitability.

Many had already experienced or witnessed attack from the air during the Zeppelin or Gotha raids of the earlier hostilities and had no wish to repeat this. A sub-committee set up under Sir John Anderson in May 1924 had concluded that London would be targeted at once in the event of war with horrifying casualties. The bombing of Barcelona during the Spanish Civil War provided a further source for concern and commentators such as Bertrand Russell and the writer and politician Harold Nicolson wrote privately of the likelihood of massive fatalities, pandemonium and 'perhaps riot' in the event of a similar attack on London. But the populace remained generally unaware of such predictions and, despite the recognised certainty that high explosives would be the main weapon of destruction, early civil defence preparations concentrated almost exclusively on the threat of gas.

An early sign of preparations in Upminster came in early January 1938 when the front page of the *Hornchurch and Upminster News* carried a picture of Mr Howard, superintendent of the Upminster and Hornchurch St John's Ambulance Brigade, giving instructions to members on the use of gas masks and protective clothing at an anti-gas demonstration at Upminster. Towards the end of March 1938 with 'the danger of war becoming more real each day' Hornchurch Council convened a special public meeting, announcing the appointment of an air raid precaution officer and launching an appeal for volunteers. The appeal met with little response locally. Of the 2,800 volunteers who had been sought, just 300 enrolled by the start of September 1938: 150 for the 1,200 air raid warden vacancies; 80 against 730 needed to provide first aid; only 9 of the 140 drivers needed; and 36 of 250 auxiliary firemen sought. In additions there were 300 vacancies for support staff such as typists, telegraphists, clerks and storekeepers, and 250 needed for the police service. A major recruiting drive was planned during October 1938.

But events moved quickly during September 1938 and the public apathy which marked the preceding months was replaced by an urgent need to make up for lost time as a general belief grew that war was about to break out. Volunteers crowded into ARP stations, while in the local parks a series of pattern trenches were dug, not for general use but for the use of any civilian caught in the open during an air raid. The Essex Education Committee agreed that schools in Upminster and other vulnerable local areas should be closed as soon as war broke out and the children evacuated to safer outlying parts of the country. Parents were called to a meeting on Wednesday 28 September and given forms to complete for each child who should 'be provided with a change of clothing, a mackintosh or overcoat and food for a journey'. That same day Upminster's peace was disturbed by the loud hoot of an air raid siren mounted on the police station roof being tested to establish the best means of alerting all in the parish. Although deafening to those in the village centre it was 'little more than a faint whine' at Corbets Tey.

Initially the need to equip all parishioners with gas masks was thwarted – no masks had been obtained and supplies had to be rushed from Cambridge and assembled rapidly. Issuing started on Sunday 25 September when 20,000 were fitted in the Urban District, but a halt was called when the numbers needed, some 90,000, failed to materialise, with a shortfall of at least 30,000 reported: it was later said that there was 'a state of panic at the fittings at schools'. Many believed war had been declared – a quarter of the crowd streaming out of the Capitol Cinema in St Mary's Lane on the evening of Saturday 24 were said to be in this position. Local traders were hard hit as they found that their customers were unwilling to spend in the same way as normally as the threat of war escalated.

Prime Minster Chamberlain was intent on averting war at any price: on 28 September 1938 he flew to Munich to meet Hitler and other heads of government. On his return to London, apprehensive Upminster residents and local business people, whose conversation had been subdued throughout the day, listened intently in hushed silence to the Prime Minister's radio broadcast, fearing the worst. But Chamberlain had come back with a document which signified 'peace in our time' and war was averted for the time being.

In Upminster, as elsewhere, the lack of preparations were evident for all to see. Had war broken out at the end of September fewer than half would have had gas masks, there were practically no adequately protected air raid shelters, while ARP volunteers had yet to attend their first lecture on what to do. Most saw the Munich agreement as offering at best a breathing space: certainly the local builders, merchants and contractors must have reached this conclusion

Recreation Ground, Upminster.

Upminster's Recreation Ground: In May 1939 demonstration air-raid shelters were erected and after the war started it was dug up to build an underground air-raid trench.

as the following week a full page of advertisements appeared in the local paper offering materials and instructions on how to build an air raid shelter. Chamberlain's words were treated with healthy scepticism, and the Munich crisis had shaken Britain out of complacency.

But little sign of ARP activity was evident in March 1939 and when some action was taken in April 1939 it resembled pure farce: volunteers wardens were told on Thursday 30 March to attend a meeting the next day, at which they were ordered to attend St Mary's Lane School on Saturday morning, appropriately 1 April, to collect respirators or distribution. This required Senior Wardens to collect between 300 and 500 boxes, make arrangements to transport them away and store them, and to assemble the boxes and pack the respirators – in the words of one warden this 'thankless task' was willingly carried out, despite 'no facilities from the local authority'.

Some progress was evident by May 1939. On 5 May some seventy-five Upminster wardens of K Group took part in an exercise to familiarise themselves with the methods of reporting damage and in a similar exercise in June 1939 J Group were expected to cope with the effects of 'bombs' which 'fell' throughout Upminster at twenty sites. Also in May the council erected air shelters in the Recreation Ground for demonstration purposes and by July two concrete wardens' posts were to be seen, one at the junction of Aylett Road and Howard Road, the other near the Bridge House, the first of sixty or seventy planned for the Hornchurch UDC area. The local ARP wardens took part in a national exercise on the night of 9/10 August 1939 during the hours of darkness under which a four-hour blackout was proposed. Despite the low and dense cloud cover the local group went ahead, dealing with 46 'incidents' throughout the area such as assumed bombs at 62 Hall Lane, 19 Engayne Gardens and many other local addresses. As war approached, on 1 September notices were pasted up in prominent places around the district giving advice about how to act in the event of air raid warnings.

At 11.15 am on Sunday 3 September 1939 the Prime Minister Neville Chamberlain announced to the nation that this country was at war with Germany. No sooner had he finished speaking than the awful wail of the air raid sirens was heard in Upminster and surrounding districts. At 9 Garbutt Road the shock was too much for Mrs Emily Bone, seventy-seven-year-old former cook to the Joslin family, who was preparing her mid-day meal when the alert sounded. Suddenly struck down by a stroke she died soon afterwards, becoming Upminster's first civilian casualty of the hostilities, albeit indirectly. Like many alerts over the next few years it was occasioned by a false alarm, triggered by a stray French aircraft which had flown over an observation post at Maidstone.

Nearly a year passed before a real threat from Nazi Germany challenged Upminster's borders. During the so-called 'phoney war', which tentatively marked the first twelve months of the conflict, Britain's air defences were not tested by the *Luftwaffe*. But a range of measures were introduced which significantly affected day-to-day life. Air raid wardens' posts were staffed and wardens were entitled to one free meal every 24 hours at a café near the Commemoration Hall at the Congregational church, where most were stationed. Public trenches accommodating 300 people were dug 7ft below ground in the Recreation Ground. Lined with six-inch concrete walls and covered with earth, ventilation was by glazed earthenware pipes which protruded some 15 inches above ground, providing a ready target for local boys' stone throwing! All road direction signs were removed, as well as railway station names and any other signs on premises which carried the name of the place. Wire cables were erected on steel poles over the Southend Arterial Road and other main routes which might be used by enemy aircraft as landing runways while, to reduce the possible effect of flying shattered glass, railway carriage windows were lined with a stout lining glued to the internal face. A blackout, introduced as a precautionary step two days before the formal declaration of hostilities, was imposed. Not only were all house and building windows to be obscured but car headlights were also prohibited except through narrow slits in covering hoods, while side lights and rear lights also needed to be obscured. Despite the initial lack of enemy action, the blackout was scrupulously enforced by the ARP wardens, sometimes to the disdain of the population at large.

Local schools were closed while men were hard at work on site 'completing trenches and other forms of protection against air-raids'. By the end of October

1939 schools had still not reopened and children received tuition in the form of 'glorified homework' which teachers issued for them to complete at home to be returned the next day. Schools were finally reopened towards the end of November 1939 although attendance was poor: no doubt the severe winter weather and the fact that the shelters at Gaynes School, for instance, were not completed until May 1940 had each played a part. Those pupils who attended school did not always follow a normal timetable: in early June 1940 many classes at Gaynes were engaged in writing ration books, some 16,000 being completed by 17 June.

By the end of 1939 a number of green-painted wooden huts with white roofs had been erected at the edge of the Recreation Ground for use as first aid posts and decontamination centres. For the local tradesmen one local benefit of war was that local people were more inclined to do their Christmas shopping in Upminster rather than travelling to London.

The first local action came on 22 May 1940 when an allied forces' Hampden bomber, piloted by PO Elmer Coton, limping back to England after a failed bombing raid on Germany in which its three-man crew had baled out, came under fire from British guns based at Hornchurch Aerodrome. PO Coton himself parachuted from his plane, watching it crash to earth just across the borders of Upminster at Berwick Road, Rainham.

The initial British setback of the war and the enforced major evacuation of the British Expeditionary Force from Dunkirk at the end of May and early June 1940 led to the need to 'house' the returning troops. A number of homes in Upminster had been empty since their owners and occupiers had been evacuated by their employers to areas 'safer' from aerial bombardment, principally the West Country, Wales and the North East. Following Dunkirk, army personnel under the authority of Brigadier Lennox Boyd descended on the parish and gained entry to larger unoccupied houses, principally in the Hall Lane area, initially for occupation by troops of the Lowland Regiment. This was regularised after the event by serving Requisition Notices (and collecting keys) for the most part to Gates & Son of Station Road, acting as agents for the respective owners. It transpired that a schedule of vacant houses had been prepared by the local police a week or two in advance on the pretext that it would be of assistance in the event of severe bomb damage or destruction and would avoid the need to search for 'trapped' occupiers. Police Sergeant Marshall, present with Brigadier Lennox Boyd, appeared in a friendly way amused at the discomfort of the agents at being caught unawares, until rebuked with the comment 'What's the joke Sergeant?' Hacton House, then also vacant, was taken over for use as the company headquarters. The Lowland Regiment was subsequently moved on to be replaced by other troops and army uniforms became a common sight in Upminster.

The German aerial onslaught on Britain began on 10 July 1940, as the first stage of the planned invasion of these shores. Their aim was to gain

Unoccupied houses in the Hall Lane area were requisitioned by the Army in 1940.

air supremacy and therefore RAF airfields were specifically singled out for attention, with bases at North Weald and Debden bombed 16 August. Eight days later on 24 August Hornchurch Air Field was on the receiving end of its first attack, with over eighty bombs falling on nearby south Hornchurch and Rainham. One of the aggressors, a Heinkel 111 bomber, was disabled by anti-aircraft fire and became an easy target for two fighters, forcing it down at Clay Tye Hill, North Ockendon, again just outside Upminster's boundaries. Two days later, at 3.15 pm on 29 August, came the first direct effect on the parish itself, again from a forced landing. Sergeant Edward Prchal, a Czech pilot serving with the RAF, based at Duxford, crashed his badly damaged Hurricane fighter in a field near to Cranham Hall. Scavenging from downed planes by souvenir hunters was rife and one Frederick Major, an Upminster baker's roundsman, was later caught with a complete machine gun from the plane in his baker's van, for which he was fined £4.

For the next two weeks Upminster continued to avoid the direct impact of the German attack. Although there were two local incidents, both were again caused by crashing planes – one British, one German. The first of these came on 30 August when Sergeant Ian Hutchinson, attempting to return to his Hornchurch base, crash-landed his Spitfire at Damyns Hall Farm, Warwick Lane. A week later, 7 September, a Messerschmitt BF110 fighter, escorting bombers in the German daylight raid on London which marked the beginning of a new phase of their strategy – the Blitz – was attacked and shot down by three British fighters. Both pilot and gunner/radio operator baled out but failed to survive while their aircraft came down at Park Corner Farm, Hacton Lane. Some forty-four years later in September 1984 the site was excavated by members of the Essex Historical Aircraft Society and one of the most impressive finds, one of the two V12 Daimler-Benz engines, can now be seen at the Aviation Museum at Coat House Fort, Tilbury.

It was inevitable with the escalating German attacks on the capital, initially both night and day but as aircraft losses mounted soon restricted to the hours of darkness only, that Upminster's charmed existence would soon be brought to an end. In the early hours of 10 September what is now the Havering area received its first serious attention from the *Luftwaffe*. Upminster's first bombing incidents were an unexploded bomb at Cranston Park Avenue and a barn at Pooles farm set alight by incendiaries. The first significant raids causing damage to property and, sadly, loss of life came within two weeks, during which time surrounding areas had already been badly affected. Just after 1 am on 23 September 1940 a bomb fell partly on and adjacent to houses in Corbets Tey Road but failed to explode on impact. Residents in the immediate area were immediately evacuated, fortunately with no injuries. While waiting to be rendered safe the bomb exploded of its own accord during the mid-morning of the following day, demolishing four houses, including Nos. 151 and 153, with severe damage to those adjoining. On this occasion the blast seems to have been smothered and there was only a minimum of surrounding damage.

Park Corner Farm was destroyed by enemy bombs on 5 October 1940.

Almost 24 hours later on Monday 24 September 1940 an elderly Upminster couple were not so fortunate. Robert Williams and Fanny Mortlock, both seventy years old, of Victoria Row Cottages, St Mary's Lane, became Upminster's first civilian fatalities, falling victims to a high explosive bomb. Three of those in neighbouring cottages were injured but survived, while others nearby escaped injury, including Mr & Mrs Carson, over eighty years of age, whose cottage adjoining those demolished was so severely damaged that the structure proved to be dangerous. As ARP workers were busy at the scene another bomb exploded in a nearby field, causing them to dive to the ground. Fortunately they were unharmed and continued their unhappy task.

Over the next few weeks came other bombing incidents causing demolitions, destruction and injury but no loss of life. The cruellest blow to Upminster's heritage came on the evening of 5 October when the sixteenth-century farmhouse of Park Corner Farm at Hacton, home to Mr & Mrs Walter John (Jack) Knight, was destroyed by enemy action.

Sunday 20 October 1940 was the most tragic night of the war so far for Upminster when at around 8pm a stick of bombs devastated parts of Waldegrave Gardens, Cranborne Gardens. Champion Road, St Mary's Lane, Sunnyside, Tudor and Derham Gardens. No. 22 Cranborne Gardens was destroyed and Mrs Irene Parker, the fifty-five-year-old postmistress was killed, although her husband and two Misses Parker who were also in the house were injured but survived. One bomb landing on the hard footpath and road surface at the junction of Tudor and Derham Gardens destroyed properties in Tudor Gardens and extensively damaged those in Derham Gardens. At 34 Tudor Gardens Mr Charles Tipping and his wife Ethel were buried under the debris of their house: Mr Tipping was rescued, but badly injured, while his sixty-year-old wife had been killed. Mr P. Flanagan who was passing by in the road when the bomb went off was injured but had a lucky escape. The bomb in St Mary's Lane fell in the entrance of the infants' school, wrecking the cloakrooms but leaving the rest of the building without heavy damage. While repairs to the school were being carried out four classes from the junior school were accommodated at Gaynes School.

Upminster fared better over the weeks that followed this shattering evening, although a few stray incidents occurred, including the bombing of a wing of Gaynes School on 8 November 1940 in a raid which saw other damage to property and injuries to residents. The Gaynes school keeper Mr H.C. (Bert) Burnham and his wife had a very lucky escape because on that night they changed their usual practice of sleeping under the floor of the raised hall (now the stage). The bomb fell on the south-east corner of the second hall (now the stage or dining area) wrecking most of it and damaging two classrooms. The school was closed for ten days.

Bomb damage to the hall at Gaynes School, November 1940.

Before dawn on the morning of 21 November, No. 48 Tawny Avenue received a direct hit from a German bomb which demolished it. Mrs Nelly Bellett died instantly when the bomb exploded in the room in which she was sleeping, but the other occupants Mr & Mrs Clark survived. Next door the Gilbert family escaped virtually intact – one member, sixty-two-year-old Miss Pike was unhurt despite falling with her room into the bomb crater.

After the Tawny Avenue tragedy Upminster escaped fairly lightly over the following two months which saw the main thrust of the German attacks change to dropping incendiaries instead of high explosive and their targets increasingly took in areas outside the capital, which experienced a respite from the intensity of the bombing of autumn 1940. March 1941 saw a renewal of the Blitz but again there were only isolated incidents, none causing casualties. An intensive raid on London on 10 May 1941 marked the turning point, after which the skies over Upminster were relatively quiet for almost three years.

It was around this time in May 1941 that a new dimension came to Upminster's war. A remote site at Gerpins Lane on the edges of the parish was requisitioned from its owners the Walker Sand and Ballast Company for the use of the RAF's 6221 Bomb disposal flight. A Nissen Hut was erected on site for the convenience of the airmen occupied on these dangerous duties, whose main food and accommodation was at RAF Hornchurch. The so-called 'Upminster Bomb Cemetery' was also used by army bomb disposal units. The RAF unit transferred to another part of the gravel pit in 1947 and their task of making safe unexploded bombs continued until 1959, when the site reverted to the ownership of the sand and gravel company. Today, of course, the site is now the London Borough of Havering's Corporation Refuse Tip.

The relative peace from air raids lasted until 21 January 1944, when a renewed and bloody German onslaught brought a new phase of the conflict. Early the next morning Howard Road experienced damage from a British anti-aircraft shell fired at the raiders who had caused destruction and death at Romford Brewery and other areas nearby. Death returned to Upminster two weeks later on the morning of 4 February with the death of an air raid warden, Frank Garwood, a fifty-five-year-old part-time warden, who was carrying out his duties outside his warden's post in the grounds of Branfil School, Cedar Avenue, only opened five months previously. The impact of a high explosive bomb which landed close by in the middle of the road demolished four bungalows, heaped debris on the warden's post and sent a bomb splinter which mortally wounded the popular warden. Just feet away inside the concrete warden's post his wife Miriam was also on duty as a warden: she was unhurt and despite her husband's death bravely continued at her post until relieved by another warden. Strangely the iron railings around the school, only feet away from the bomb crater, were not so much as bent. They also survived the scrap metal drives of the war years and can still be seen surrounding the school today.

There had been much speculation about the likelihood of a German secret weapon, a flying bomb, but the allied invasion of the European mainland, D-Day, which went ahead on 6 June 1944, took place without any signs of German reprisal. Seven days later on 13 June the first V1 flying bombs were launched, two of which reached these shores, although it was several weeks before the authorities admitted their existence. The attack began in earnest on the night of 15/16 June when seventy-three 'doodlebugs', as they came to be known, reached London. What is now the Havering area was hit by seven of the Nazi's secret weapon, causing twice that number of fatalities; one fell in the Upminster area but there was no damage and nobody was injured. Over the next two weeks the local area again suffered but Upminster remained intact until the morning of 1 July when a V1 came down on two pairs of vacant houses of flat-roof construction in Tawny Avenue and were fragmented leaving only a large crater. There was little sign of brick or rubble which appeared to have been dispersed over a wide area. The immediately adjoining houses escaped extensive damage and continued fit for occupation.

The next flying bomb to strike Upminster three weeks later proved fatal. Lilian Welch, fifty-six, and her twenty-two-year-old daughter Kathlyn of 51 Springfield Gardens died when a flying bomb exploded in their rear garden near the shelter in which they were sleeping. Mr Welch survived as he slept in a downstairs room, as he had a few days previously been discharged from hospital after a serious operation, and his condition had stopped him going into the shelter, saving his life. Tragically his daughter, who had evacuated with her firm to another part of the country, had only arrived home for the weekend to see her father a few hours earlier. The bomb caused considerable blast damage to many houses, particularly in Sunnyside Gardens, and the scene between Springfield and Sunnyside Gardens was reminiscent of a First World War battlefield, with widespread destruction and trees stripped of leaves and branches. The local paper reported that there was some resentment as throughout the day a stream of sightseers to the scene hampered the efforts of those blast victims trying to remove their furniture from their bombed-out houses as quickly as possible.

The last of the four V1s to strike Upminster also had fatal consequences. On 7 August a flying bomb came down near the northern end of the parish, destroying three cottages and a small chapel in Hall Lane. Two days later one of the occupiers, Mrs Mary Holman, seventy-five, of Tyes Cottage, died from her injuries in Harold Wood Hospital. Elsewhere in the locality V-bombs continued to land throughout the August, with a handful continuing through to November, by which time the Allied advance had made things increasingly difficult for the Germans to use their launching sites, resorting instead to a campaign of air-launched bombs. But by that time a new terror had been inflicted on Britain – the V2 rocket. The first of these new vengeance weapons struck Chiswick at 6.40 am on 8 September 1944, followed soon after by another landing at Epping. Havering's first V2 came just over a week later on 16 September with a rocket landing in a field of corn stubble at Noak Hill; another followed in October before the assault proper began in November. Upminster lived a charmed life, surviving the new weapon of mass destruction until 20 January 1945 when the first came down in field to the rear of Argyle Gardens and west of Cranham Hall, with three serious casualties, twenty-four houses made uninhabitable and considerable damage to others. Mr and Mrs Clark, who had survived the destruction of No. 48 Tawny Avenue, had been re-housed in one of the houses immediately backing onto the field where the rocket fell. One month later on 20 February another V-bomb landed in a field at Aylens Farm, east of Hall Lane, with slight damage to only ten houses.

But the next V2 to hit Upminster was to prove the most costly in terms of loss of life and the date of 12 March 1945 – as represented by the sequence of numbers 12.3.45 – still remains firmly embedded in local memory. Like other V2s the launch of yet another German rocket would have been heralded by a blip on a screen watched by an Allied radar engineer. But knowing that another rocket was on its way was met by helpless inactivity, for there was no way of predicting exactly where the weapon would come to land, other than somewhere in the south of England. It was little consolation and a little ironic that the engineers exploiting their radar technology could identify where the rocket had been launched from on its four-minute journey. So when, at around twenty minutes after midnight on 12 March, the launch of the rocket from The Hague/Duindigt area of the Netherlands was pinpointed there was no inkling that Upminster would be on the receiving end. The seemingly random nature of the V2 attacks meant that most people risked sleeping in their houses rather than the flimsy garden air-raid shelters. So the explosion at 00.25 that night of a V2 rocket in the front garden of No. 63 Waldegrave Gardens to the north of the railway found most occupiers of nearby houses asleep in their beds. Had the occupier of that house Mrs Watson been there the loss of life would have been greater. As it was the blast claimed five lives in the adjacent houses. At No. 61 the explosion caused two victims: Mrs Annie Lewis, forty-one, was killed along with her seven year-old son Maxwell, while her husband survived, although badly injured, along with their eleven-month-old son who was released from the debris after the rescuers heard his faint cries coming from the rubble. On the other side at No. 65 Ralph and Jessie Brooks, a married couple in their late fifties, both perished in their completely devastated home. Next door at No. 67 two year-old Richard Oakes, who had been lying in bed between his parents, lost his life while they survived, although badly injured by a falling chimney. Families living opposite had a variety of lucky escapes: a telegraph pole from outside No. 63 flew down the road and lodged itself in the bedroom wall at No. 54, narrowly missing Mr & Mrs Howes, while the occupiers of No. 50 were sucked out of the bedroom and onto their front lawn, still lying in bed. When dawn broke the extent of the devastation was evident: eleven houses, built only six or seven years before, were either destroyed or so badly damaged that they had to be completely rebuilt after the war.

Thankfully the war was nearly at an end. At least there were no more local casualties even when another V2 hit the parish five days later on 17 March, fortunately coming to ground in a field near to Brambles Farm, causing only minor damage.

A V2 rocket claimed five lives in Waldegrave gardens on 12 March 1945.

7
STATION ROAD AND ITS TRADERS
EAST SIDE

LIKE OTHER RURAL communities Upminster depended on a number of small village traders who could feed, clothe, equip and provide services for its population. With its inhabitants clustered in hamlets at Corbets Tey, Hacton and towards Upminster Common, as well as in the village centre and along the main through-route, which later became known as St Mary's Lane, a single grouping of shops and services was not practicable. Each of the far-spread communities was usually able to meet many of its essential urgent needs from a local shop. Corbets Tey in particular was well served, at least by public houses, having no less than three until the 1890s!

In the early years of the century the village centre and nearby area offered the full range of shops serving day-to-day needs with a butcher, a baker, a drapers, grocers and post office, and other traders. With W.P. Griggs and Co.'s development of the garden suburb from 1906 onwards there was an evident need for more substantial shopping parades to meet the needs of the new residents and to encourage others to follow. The developers no doubt felt that a block of purpose-built shops in a modern setting would be a fitting part of their plans and without too much delay work began on the chosen site within close proximity of the station, on the east side of Station Road running north from Howard Road. Another parade soon followed between St Lawrence Road and Howard Road. These two parades housed retail units on the ground floor with two floors of residential accommodation above, ideal for a husband and wife team running a family business, as was commonplace at the time.

THE APPROACH

This provided access from Station Road to the original station entrance, booking hall and Station Master's house, together with the Goods Bay Parcel Office and, further east, to the sidings. A subway connected the up and down platforms and the Romford/Grays branch line but this ceased to be of practical use after the District Line extension in 1932 when the booking hall was moved on to the bridge, which was widened to its now-existing width.

Near the entrance to The Approach coal order offices were sited, controlling the purchase of coal stocks and retailing these to local residents. Coal mined in the north of England and loaded into open-topped trucks at pit side was transported by rail, and off-loaded at specific coal bays of retailers, where it was weighed into hundredweight coal bags and delivered to customers, all for two shillings and sixpence per cwt., winter price or two shillings and three pence 'lowest summer price'.

From as early as 1899 through to at least 1916 Daldy & Co. were listed as coal merchants at the station; by 1926 W.H. Sproul & Co., in the ownership of William Chisnell and for a time Harwin & Saunders, were operating such a business. Others listed in this trade at the station at various times were Charrington, Gardner, Locket & Co. (Charringtons), Adams & Gates, and T.A. & C. Abrahams (the millers of Upminster Mill who also operated a coal supply business).

Messrs Miller and Langdon outside E. N. Selby's premises in Station Approach, *c.* 1928.

Timber buildings on the south side of The Approach were used in the late 1920s and early 1930s by Ernest N. Selby, Auctioneer & Estate Agent, whose father was the builder and developer of the early part of Cranham in Front Lane and the connecting roads south of the railway bridge. The estate office was doubtless for the purpose of encouraging property sales in the then developing area of Cranham. E.N. Selby later moved to No. 54 Station Road. Hamilton Boulton, estate agent, was also located in The Approach, ceasing business in the mid-1930s.

HOWARD ROAD TO STATION APPROACH

This parade was built to a high specification with a front elevation of part brick and part stone, positioned to allow a wide forecourt – a departure from the more common location of shops close to the public footpath. The following list has been drawn up from surviving records, or else the information is within memory from the 1920s or early 1930s.

No. 70 Station Road

This site alongside The Approach – now The Yeoman public house – was originally owned by the railway company. Alfred Rendle established his nurseryman's and florist's business in a lock-up shop at 'Station Corner' around 1921, as an outlet for his nursery in Nags Head Lane, H. Stanley Pudney, FRHS, succeeding him around 1927, remaining there until around 1963.

Looking south around 1930. Nearly all the shops in this parade have remained in the same trade since they opened in 1907.

No. 68 Station Road

The shops from 60 to 68 are unusual in that from the time that the parade was built around 1907 they have all stayed in the same trade for eighty-nine years. This premise has been continuously a wine and spirit merchants or off-licence; the proprietor through into the 1920s was Joseph William Turner before the Victoria Wine Company took over.

No. 66 Station Road

This shop has also stayed in the same trade, namely as a bakery. Mark Albert Wheeler was the original proprietor before Henry Frizzell succeeded him around the First World War in what became very much a family business, engaging his son Howard and his daughters. A bake-house was situated at the rear of the main building. Daily delivery rounds were operated as standard practice but home deliveries were discontinued during the Second World War and were not re-introduced. Taken over by F.R. Murray and Son as an extension of their main bakery at Grays, this proprietorship continued until the retirement of Alan Murray. Until recently the shop continued as a bakery known as 'Windy Millers' but was out of use during the first half of 1996, before being re-opened in early August as a Kingcott's bakery, retaining the long tradition on this site.

No. 64 Station Road

Another shop which since its inception has remained in the same trade, in this case a chemist. In turn: Ernest B. Humphreys 1907 to mid-1920s, before moving to the new shop in St Mary's Lane near the school; John B. Storie during the 1930s; Ken H. Rose – who in the tradition of earlier proprietors carried on a personally run service to customers (he and his wife Renie retired to Canada to join their daughter and son-in-law – latest news is that they have five Canadian grandchildren and two great-grand-children); the business acquired by Ken Holland is now continued in the same tradition as L.S. Govani by Yakat Govani and his wife Shamin.

No. 62 Station Road

From the time that the parade was built this address appears to have housed a butcher's shop; a small abattoir was originally sited at the rear of the main building. Recorded proprietors are: Harris in 1907, James Henry Cox 1908-23, William John Tollworthy (1923-c.1935), H.W. Hart & Son (c.1935 -?), and Frank Dyer – following his decease the shop still trades under his name. Tollworthy's were still in the era when home deliveries were made to customers by smart pony and trap, with staff standing ready to give immediate effect to customers' orders.

No. 60 Station Road

A separate building to Nos. 62-68, this was originally part of Gooderham's and Green's Stores (No. 58). A Glenny & Son, Chartered Surveyors opened a branch of their Barking business at this address in the early 1930s. The late Mr Glenny, an Upminster resident, became a well-known local person, highly respected in his profession. Following a fire at the premises in 1995 and changes within the Glenny business, 60 Station Road is now the regional centre for the company's professional services.

No. 58 Station Road

The north corner of Howard Road originally housed Gooderham's stores until the business was sold to Green Stores (Ilford) Ltd. in 1916. Green's were a company with a chain of small stores of which their Upminster store was bigger than most, including at the rear Upminster Sub-Post Office under Miss Cant.

An adjacent single-storey building flanking Howard Road served as a mail sorting office and telegraph station, manned by uniformed postmen and two telegraph boys, also in smart uniform, for whom this was often the first step to a career in the postal service. Telephones in private houses were rare for many years and a quick means of communication was to telephone the Telegraph Office who would deliver the message by hand in a sealed envelope. It also housed Upminster's first telephone exchange, established in 1922, which transferred to newly built premises in St Mary's Lane in 1929.

Green's conformed to the local early-closing day of Thursday and to provide an uninterrupted postal service a roller-shutter was drawn across the rear of the grocery area. Access to the postal section was then by an entrance in Howard Road, now bricked-up but still visible in outline. In about 1938, after petitions and much local protest, a Crown Post Office opened in premises immediately opposite, formerly Kemp's Crumpled Horn Dairy, but in recent years this has lost its status and a sub-post office has been established in Martin's newsagents and confectioners at 26 Station Road. Sports Gear, later known as Spoga-Sports, was here until the early 1990s before Whitehall Kitchens took over the premises.

Upminster's first telephone exchange was housed above Green's store and post office.

HOWARD ROAD TO ST LAWRENCE ROAD

Based on memory, conjecture and some records the traders and occupiers have included the following:

Nos. 54 and 56 Station Road

This premises, now occupied by Chandler's travel, is on the south corner of Howard Road. A two-storey building devoid of ornamentation and differing in elevation to the adjoining parade, it may well have been built to order. Once a store known as Bon Marche, later Percy Goodchild occupied a draper's store here throughout the 1920s but ceased trading around 1929/30. The store stood vacant until converted to two shops. The new occupiers were Ernest Selby, estate agent and auctioneer, who moved to No. 54 from the Station Approach, and The County of London Electric Supply Company, who opened a showroom and local office at No. 56. Selby's business was subsequently incorporated with Gates, Parish & Co., while the CLESCO premises were transferred to larger premises in Corbets Tey Road. The late Harry Chandler, who in 1936 had founded and operated his Upminster travel agency for many years from his family home in Springfield Court, acquired Nos. 54 & 56, restoring the ground floor to a single unit and adding the three floor extension to the rear to control his world-wide operations.

No. 52 Station Road

The parade, now Nos. 30 to 52 Station Road, was originally numbered 1 to 12 Station Road until at least 1929, at which time the shops between Cosy Corner (see below) and St Lawrence Road acquired numbers for the first time. Built by April 1908 this parade probably followed the building of the grander parade to the north of Howard Road.

At No. 52 one of the original traders in this parade, Mr Copley the iron-monger who originated from Bow, was much loved for his dry humour and eccentricity. Unmarried, he lived over the shop with his sister Alice and his brother-in-law, Mr Charles Moore and family. Copley had intended that the business would eventually pass to Moore and his two sons Ernest and Charles, but Ernest Moore was killed in Italy in late October 1918, just weeks before the Armistice and Charles took up the printing trade. Copley therefore soldiered on without an heir to pass the business to and during his last few years he doubtless continued trading as a matter of daily habit, coupled with the opportunity to meet people, sharing with them his reminiscences of old times, which were invariably of great interest. A purchase from Mr Copley's un-modernised shop and wide range of good quality wares would entail much rummaging below the counter, before the sought-after goods were produced to the light of day with a triumphant explanation 'One and six!' As Ted Ballard recalled, Mr Copley would frequently insist on selling customers what he felt would suit their purpose better, rather than what they may have asked for, often doing so at much less cost. Margaret Crabtree's recent book relates an amusing example of how Mr Copley declined to sell her father five inch nails when the six inch nails he asked for were out of stock, snapping that 'If you want six inch nails, five inch nails won't do. You should know that'. A kindly man of a former generation.

During 1950 Ashby Rogers & Co., solicitors, took possession with an expanded staff. The senior partner was Mr Archibald Rogers, a well-respected local resident of Engayne Gardens, who was joined by further partners Robert Gibb (in 1953), Lewis 'John' Raddon in 1957 and Gordon Bowley in 1962. They were assisted by Harry Ball in the litigation department and Reg Wingate as managing clerk. Gordon Bowley later became senior partner following the retirement of his colleagues and continued for some years until the merger with Pinney & Co. The firm now practices as Pinney Rogers, under the control of Mr Tony Allen.

No. 50 Station Road

Kemp's Crumpled Horn Dairy was sited here before this was relocated to the other side of Station Road around 1926. Kemp's was succeeded by a grocer and provisions store of the International Tea Company under the management of Mr Lake for many years from the 1930s. Mr Lake was another shopkeeper who lived over the store and together with his wife was very much part of the local community. This branch of 'International' closed at the on-set of 'out-of-town shopping', to be replaced by the 'Wimpy Bar', still in being operated by Mr S. Gill.

No. 48 Station Road

From the opening of this shopping parade in 1908 Charles Albert Davis conducted his business as a bespoke tailor here. Davis had served his apprenticeship to a Stratford tailor and his father bought the freehold of the Station Road business for him to set up on his own account. He lived in a flat over the premises and during the Second World War he was, together with Mr Searson (No. 38), the co-ordinator of the fire-watchers' rota in Station Road. In the city of London the lack of such precautions outside working hours had resulted in unreported fires from incendiary bombs, which contributed to the widespread destruction in the city in 1940. Such rotas were then made compulsory in business areas. The premises were later occupied by Mr Geoffrey Vitoria and a tailor's business is now continued by Mr J. Cooper.

Charles Davis outside his tailor's shop, 48 Station Road.

NOS. 44 AND 46 STATION ROAD

Mr Neam Bennett, assisted by his wife, operated a hardware and domestic store at No. 44, living over the premises. They appear to have succeeded Mrs Ellen Reeves who ran a china and glass merchants from this address. By around 1945/46 the Bennetts themselves had been succeeded by Mayes in the same line of business. Ron Dobson had, in 1933, established in St Mary's Lane a hardware and domestic store coupled with the sale of hand tools. A progressive trader with a concentration on service to customers, he was offered Mayes' business at 44 Station Road, taking possession in 1960. Dobson and Co., by then including his sons, acquired the adjoining property of 46 Station Road. Over a highly concentrated few days the party wall was removed to double the size of the well-appointed premises in which to extend the range of merchandise. The large display area now includes china, glassware, gifts, domestic hardware and sundry items.

Before being acquired by Dobson & Co., No. 46 had been operated for a variety of uses. In 1916 Leppard and Carter, cycle manufacturers, seem to have traded here and later E.C. Carter alone ran a motor business. Carter appears to have been superseded by Amy Marshall and Miss V. Patrick, who each traded in the early and late 1920s respectively as ladies outfitters. In the late 1930s this address briefly housed Thomas Moy's coal merchants sales office and in later years was in turn a wool shop and retailer of ladies wear. Subsequently it was operated by Mrs Anglin and her son and later, Mr C.L. Taylor. The present occupier John Dobson recalls that before they could proceed with the renovation they needed to replace the ground floor plaster ceilings which were impregnated with the smell of fish.

No. 42 Station Road

A 'fancy repository' seems to have occupied this shop from the earliest days, with William Lowe listed in 1916. Mrs Gladys Bolton is shown as occupier in 1922 but from the mid-1920s Sydney Bolton – no doubt a relation – and his wife traded under the title The Bonanza. This shop was a veritable Aladdin's cave, and as an added attraction to their trade a large glass-fronted display cabinet, some 10ft square, was sited on the forecourt. The business closed in 1939 and this occasion was marked by a final sale to make way for Hilbery Chaplin, estate agents and surveyors; now the office of ABACUS (Insurance & Finance Consultants Ltd).

No. 40 Station Road

From the earliest days this building contained a variety of users:

Ground floor: occupied until 1921 by Ernest Watkins senior as a barber's shop (as they were then known) the freehold was acquired by E.R.H. Gates (see No. 32 below). The adjoining half-shop (40a) in the possession of the Misses Hawkes traded as 'Maison Chocolat' confectioner and tobacconist (E.B. Gates later married the younger Miss Hawkes). The goodwill of their business was acquired in the mid-1930s by Jack Bassett, who also had a similar business in Corbets Tey Road. Now restored as a single unit in the trade of newsagent/tobacconist/confectioner, together with greeting cards, under the proprietorship of Mr J. Patel.

Upper floors: from the 1920s in the occupation of Ashby, Rogers & Co., solicitors, as an offshoot of their London office at 105 Newington Causeway. The limited legal work only required the attendance of Mr A.W. Rogers each weekday evening and one mid-week afternoon. After the company moved to 52 Station Road the enlarged upper floors became the offices of S.H. Lansdell & Sons Ltd., builders responsible for Gates, Parish & Co. for over 500 new dwellings in Upminster, Cranham, West Horndon and the surrounding district; they were also builders of Willow Parade, Cranham. Now in the occupation of Mr Roger Morse, a partner of Darcy White & Co., solicitor.

Detached building at rear: origin uncertain but occupied in the late 1920s by a hand laundry. Left untenanted, apart from use as storage for estate agents' signboards, the lease was granted in 1933 to Percy Scott and Charles Brech who started trading as Upminster Printing Company. In addition to establishing a successful printing works, from July 1934 they published the weekly local paper, the *Upminster Chronicle*, surviving copies of which can be viewed at the Essex Record Office. The building at the rear of No. 30 became an office and retail outlet. On the death of Charles Brech and the retirement of Percy Scott the business has continued since 1986 with an increasing concentration on the stationery retail section under the present proprietor, Ron Manger, assisted by his wife Joyce. Collectively a valuable service to Upminster traders and residents.

No. 38 Station Road

What was to be the longest-standing business on Station Road, Searson's Boot & Shoe Retailers, was opened by Mr Herbert Searson on 2 April 1908, as he felt that opening on 1 April was chancing providence. Trading in partnership with his brother, the business was highly respected; in later years it was run by his stepson Tom Black. Mr Searson is recalled by older residents as having a withered left hand and wearing a dark suit and starched collar. Miss Ball, a resident of South Ockendon, spent the whole of her working life as chief assistant and towards retirement was the longest-serving member of the then working community in Station Road. Following the closure of the business in the late 1980s the premises were converted to house a television and hi-fi centre occupied by Mr M. Patel.

A familiar picture of Upminster 'market' in 1908, months after the parade opened. Searson's continued here until the later 1980s.

No. 36 Station Road

A wet and dried fishmonger occupied this site. Possibly originally William Rice, of Thompson and Rice, followed by Fosters and Miss Mavis Candler around 1922, in turn succeeded from the early 1920s by Arthur Rumsey, who continued in this trade until the early post-war years. A change of use to greengrocer and fruiterer followed the transfer of ownership to his son-in-law Harry Brewer and his wife Olive. The goodwill passed to 'Spicers' who traded for some years. The shop was subsequently divided into two units: currently the greengrocers and fruiterers has continued under the trade name Jeanettes in one section, with a florist, Upminster Flowers, adjoining.

No. 34 Station Road

Occupied from its opening in 1908 as a fruiterers and greengrocers by Harry Talbot, older brother of A.E. Talbot, garage proprietor. Harry Talbot retired in the early 1930s and the premises were acquired by Eric Day, whose practice as an optician was established within the ground floor by 1933. The first floor was also converted to professional use about the same time by Ivor Williams, Dental Surgeon. Day retired to New Zealand and the practice was continued by Hawkes and Stender, followed by Victor Stender on his own account. When he moved to Leigh-on-Sea a change to retail use occurred. The dental practice was run during the war years by Mr Boosey and he was rejoined in 1945 by Mr Williams, who as a commissioned army officer had gained vast experience in dental and facial operations on injured servicemen; within a few years of his return he had moved to a specialist practice in London. His successor Ron Green continued the high standards of his predecessors and became a highly respected member of the local community until his retirement, sadly living only a few years afterwards. Roy Joffe has since continued and enlarged the practice and perpetuates the service highly valued by the local community over the years.

No. 32 Station Road

Some older inhabitants may no doubt recall Miss Rhoda Leany's confectioner's which had operated here from before the First World War, although Kelly's 1937 *Essex Directory* lists Miss Alma Davis as the occupier in this trade. Photographs show the name of the shop as The Bazaar. It was vacated at the outbreak of war in 1939 and requisitioned by the army in 1940 and used as an army store. It emerged in 1945 a worn and battered building which presented a sorry sight – shop windows and other windows broken by bomb blast and boarded up, stair-treads worn wafer-thin by the hard tread of army boots, stair balusters and areas of floor boards missing. It was acquired by Gates and Son and within the limits of materials available

E. B. ('Tiny') Gates in the early 1940s with Mrs Gates *(left)* and Mrs Joan Parish *(right)*.

and Building Licensing Control it was restored to a limited usable extent.

Ernest Rose Holden Gates had formerly traded in High Street, Hornchurch in partnership with John Read, to whom he was related by marriage, as Read & Gates, surveyors and estate agents. In 1921 ERH Gates established a business in his own name and acquired the freehold of 40 Station Road, occupying half the ground floor. He was joined by his son Ernest Bridger Gates in 1926 and the title was changed to Gates & Son. E.B. Gates was a tall imposing man, known locally as 'Tiny' Gates. He lived at Brae Banks, St Mary's Lane, now part of the Carlton Close development.

ERH Gates had retired in 1929, and his son retired also in 1935, partly on health grounds, at which point a company was formed – Gates & Son Ltd. In 1935 Albert George Parish, who in 1930 had joined the firm at a wage of 12s 6d per week after leaving school, became one of the four directors. The firm continued through the war years but in 1945 Albert Parish took sole control – Hubert Cardnell retired, Robert Langdon died in action, and David Williams also retired. A change of name to Gates, Parish & Co. was accompanied by a transfer to No. 32 from their previous office at No. 40.

Soon after the war Albert Parish was joined in the practice by Leonard Collett and Gerard Williams, chartered surveyors, and in the late 1940s by his brothers John William and Leonard Charles Parish. Collett and Williams left during the 1960s to pursue their careers and in 1968 David Parish, Albert's son, a qualified chartered surveyor, joined the firm. In 1975 he succeeded his father as sole principal. J.W. Parish died in 1970 and L.C. Parish in 1990, four years after his retirement. Albert Parish continued to attend the office each day as a consultant to the firm until his sudden death on 13 March 1996 aged eighty-one, after an unbroken spell of sixty-six years working for the firm in Station Road.

The firm, celebrating their 75th anniversary in 1996, has had a major influence on the development of the area, as selling agents for many new properties, surveyors to many developers and advisers to estate design and other aspects.

No. 30 Station Road

On the north corner of St Lawrence Road the earliest occupiers were Alfred Wooff's dining rooms and teashop. Later Gillings & Co. ran a retail wall-paper, paint and decorating materials business there. Joseph Gillings, who died in 1924, had founded a decorators' business in Wanstead Park Road, Ilford in 1887, working with Thomas Donald on the Woodgrange Park Estate and working for W.P. Griggs & Co. on the Upminster garden suburb from July 1907. Gillings' company occupied No. 30 Station Road until the late 1930s.

The larger part of the first floor was the hairdressing saloon first established by Ernest Watkins senior at 40 Station Road and subsequently run by his son of the same name. After Gillings ceased their retail business, a variety of trades occupied No. 30 including Suitall valetting and a '60 minute' cleaning service immediately pre-war. In the immediate post-war years there was a down-market second-hand furniture dealer whose sundry wares spread out over the forecourt was out of character for Upminster. To the relief of many Ernie Watkins junior moved his hairdressing business to the rear ground floor, coupled with a high-class confectioner and tobacco retailers to the front shop section. Hairdressing has continued to the present day, currently with Paul's under the proprietorship of Paul Lexton.

Station Road *c.* 1920 showing Kemp's original 'Crumpled Horn Dairy'. In the background a herd of cows is turning into Battson's dairy, at the rear of No. 28.

REAR OF NO. 30 STATION ROAD

This building fronting St Lawrence Road was used originally for the storage of building plant and materials by Gillings & Co. It has passed through various uses, including a small motor garage, proprietor Mr Drew (who married a member of the Talbot family) and a furniture depository by Charles Neale, then a well-known furniture remover. The stationery section of Upminster Printing Company was opened as an extension of the company printing works at the rear of No. 40 (see above).

ST LAWRENCE ROAD TO ST MARY'S LANE

The shops and premises between St Lawrence Road and the junction with St Mary's Lane predated the development of the Edwardian garden suburb, mainly originating as private homes, and only being converted to retail uses in the later 1930s and subsequently. The east side of Station Road between Cranham Road, as it then was, and what became St Lawrence Road, was not owned by the Branfill family and for a variety of reasons was developed earlier than land in the Branfill's ownership. In April 1996 David Parish, Principal of Gates Parish, announced that a developer had approached some of his clients and freeholders of other premises in this part of Station Road with a view to the development of a major food superstore on the site on Nos. 14 to 28 and on land in St Lawrence Road. At the time of writing firm proposals for a development of this kind, which will arouse considerable local debate, have yet to be brought forward.

The original premises southwards from St Lawrence Road were as follows:

NO. 28 STATION ROAD

No. 26 (now Martin's) and 28 (now Morton & Reeves) are part of a pair of semi-detached houses built around 1886. Now in the occupation of Stanley Reeves (Morton & Reeves), a high-class grocery store and delicatessen, No. 28 seems from the outset to have been the home and business premises of Edwin Battson, dairyman, listed there in the 1891 census. Following the death of Mr Battson around the end of the First World War, the business continued as Battson Brothers who operated their dairy from this outlet at the corner of St Lawrence Road. Grocery items were progressively added to the traditional sale of butters and cheese, creating a foundation for their present use. Milk deliveries twice a day, early am and late morning/early afternoon, were essential in the era before home refrigeration. Initially transported in bulk in a churn mounted on a hand-pushed milk-cart, the milk was served by the half-pint ladle. To ensure accuracy of the measure housewives adopted glass jugs with engraved measurements on the side to deter enthusiastic roundsmen motivated by profit. Delivery progressed to specially built two-wheel horse-drawn milk-carts to enable transport of a greater volume of produce and an increased speed of round.

From about 1930 the business passed to United Dairies Ltd. to create a further branch of their extensive coverage of the outer London area. United Dairies' horses were well cared for and groomed in their stables at the rear of the store in St Lawrence Road, now the site of Roomes Apart bedding centre and customer car park. Blue stable bricks are still to be seen on the immediate position of the stables.

To the rear of 28 Station Road, fronting St Lawrence Road, other users included Mr Lewis, an electrician and a 'boffin' with a wireless. He was very much a 'professor' in the art of making and repairing sets in the early days of radio. He would collect residents' wireless accumulators and deliver them back, recharged a week later. His son Brian followed his father into the modern generation of television and hi-fi, trading as Marshalls in St Mary's Lane. Harry Hine and his two sons, plumber contractors to Upminster Estates Ltd., had their workshop and yard adjoining Mr Lewis – now the premises of Jarvo's, the fully-stocked DIY store and specially made joinery under the proprietorship of Michael Jarvis.

No. 26 Station Road

Number 26 ('Meadow View') was for many years in residential use until Arthur Dale moved there from Gaynes Road around the end of the First World War. Mr Dale – a bald-headed man usually sporting a flat cap and known to the locals as 'Diddly' Dale – conducted his news agency from the front room of his semi-detached house, unrecognisable from its modern appearance, approached from the public footpath through a gate into a front garden still surrounded by fencing. It was a true example of the progression to trading use of residential premises to cater for an expanding population. Assisted by his wife and daughter, he unfailingly greeted his customers in a friendly way, in keeping with the village atmosphere still existing at the time.

Acquired by David Alexander Ramsay in 1940, in addition to his existing premises at 203 St Mary's Lane, the fencing was removed and a forecourt laid. The later installation of a shop front was in keeping with the changing face of Station Road. The scope of the business was widened as Miss Ramsay progressively took over from her father, leading to the business in its current form. The present occupiers Martin McColls operate from an enlarged ground floor, which now includes a sub-post office, following the closure of the main office at 55/57 Station Road.

Nos. 22 and 24 Station Road

Known as 'Oakhurst', No. 22 was probably built in the late 1880s, along with the adjoining house of 'Elmhurst' (No. 24) as the home and business premises of William Hook, builder and former partner of Upminster's historian T.L. Wilson. The premises passed into commercial use after A.E. (Albert Edward) Talbot established his wheelwright's trade there before the First World War. One of Albert's older brothers, Harry, thirteen years his senior and a former employee of Henry Joslin at Gaynes, was one of the first traders to take up a shop, a greengrocers at No. 34, in the newly built Station Road parade around 1908. No doubt this encouraged the young Albert to try his luck in the blossoming Edwardian suburb of Upminster a few years later. At first his wife Elizabeth and family lived in Barking until the wheelwright's business became established at Station Road. The firm diversified from its original wheelwrights, adding bicycles and, before 1922, family motorcars to its trade, erecting petrol pumps on the forecourt of its Station Road premises. Talbots became a family firm when Albert and Elizabeth's sons, Albert, Leonard, Walter and the present proprietor Malcolm progressively joined him in the business, which traded as A.E. Talbot and Sons. The firm's founder died in February 1963, aged eighty-two, outliving his wife by some ten years.

Albert Edward Talbot, born in September 1880 at Great Thurlow, Suffolk, and his wife Elizabeth née Missen.

For many years another, more unusual, service offered by Talbots was to provide garage facilities in a shed in the work yard for the parish council's fire engine, both the manual appliance and the solid-tyred Model 'T' Ford engine which replaced it, before alternative garaging was acquired in the stables as part of the Clockhouse in St Mary's Lane, in the mid-1920s.

Oakhurst had been bought in 1923, along with the adjacent Elmhurst, occupied by the Caldecourts, who opened a business as plumbers, gas fitters and glaziers etc. John Richard Caldecourt and his wife Lilly lived at 'Elmhurst' from the 1890s, with their ten children – five girls and five boys, two of whom died in the First World War and are listed on Upminster's war memorial. John, who died in 1926, was a plumber and glazier; his son Ernie continued the business concentrating on the plumbing trade. Another son, Ted, operated a decorator's business from the same address. After the Caldecourt family moved to Gaynes Road, Elmhurst stood vacant until taken over by the Home Guard during the Second World War. Later Talbot & Sons expanded to take over the neighbouring Elmhurst, establishing modern showrooms from the lower floor of the red brick Victorian houses. The dealership concentrated on cars of the Rootes Group, in later years coincidently coming under the Talbot brand name. It is currently a Renault dealers and service centre, the long-standing petrol business having ceased in July 1996.

Station Road looking north *c*. 1930. Talbot's garage is prominent on the right of the picture, beyond the railings of the National School building.

FORMER NATIONAL SCHOOL

The history of the National School, with its small bell-tower and adjacent schoolmaster's house built in 1850/51, has been described in detail in a later chapter. After the building of the new school in St Mary's Lane in 1928 the old National School was put to various uses, including overflow classrooms, a meeting place for local associations and a social club for young people. Attempts to extend its uses for the benefit of the community ceased prior to its demolition in 1967 to make way for the new Upminster Branch of the National Westminster Bank and two adjoining shops.

Nos. 4 to 12 Station Road

In late 1938/early 1939 former houses to the south of the National School were demolished to enable the re-development of the area behind Cosy Corner. The Cosy Corner landmark too was planned for demolition on completion of the building work but, with the intervention of war in September 1939, this was left stranded on an 'island' site forward of the building line, along for a while with the old Lloyds Bank building. The newly built parade of five shops and the bank were completed in mid-1939 and although Lloyds Bank were able to take occupation of their new premises before the outbreak of war the adjoining shops were boarded up and remained unoccupied for the duration. The self-contained residential flats on the first and second floor were occupied progressively from 1940 onwards.

The five shops re-offered for letting in 1945/46 attracted various trades, including a small furniture store; men's outfitters and shoe retailers, a branch of Souster Brothers of Ilford. In the subsequent years occupiers have changed many times and only one trade has continued – a shoe retailers, present occupiers Mr A.R. Murray.

Premises between Old National School and Cosy Corner

The first premises in Station Road was possibly originally a private house, which around 1901 was significantly enlarged to form a purpose-built shop, described on its opening as 'handsome and spacious new premises'. In March 1902 the business was transferred to Adolphus Pilcher, who in turn was succeeded around 1912 by Charles W. Jupp & Sons. Jupp continued to carry

Charles Jupp's butcher's shop which later became the premises of Lloyds Bank.

out the butcher's trade here until around 1930, when there was a significant change of use – Lloyds Bank established a branch here. Above the bank was a self-contained flat, which was the home of the bank manager. The bank building survived into the war years, after which the premises relocated into the new parade at the bank's rear.

For a while to the north of the bank was a small wooden office, from which a Miss Nunn, whose family lived in Branfill Road, operated a business selling typewriters and accessories. Upminster's historian and jack-of-all-trades, Thomas Lewis Wilson lived near here at the lower end of Station Road in America Cottage, with his builder's yard at the rear running through onto St Mary's Lane. In 1914 Wilson, then aged eighty-one, moved to Grove Cottage in St Mary's Lane and Newton H. Wilson 'builder & undertaker' took over. Not long afterwards he was succeeded by Alfred Edward Parrish, carman, who continued here into the 1930s.

Before the old Boys' School was a double-fronted house which was converted into two shops – Madam Elizabeth's, milliners and ladies clothing shop which operated in the 1920s, and a second shop of Frizzell's the bakers, which operated as a tea-shop.

COSY CORNER, NO. 137 ST MARY'S LANE

This well-known landmark, part timber-framed and part brick, had been built by 1831 by William Hammond, on what was then part of the unenclosed village green, the grant from the manor court recording in June 1831 that this was already a butcher's shop occupied by Edward Oakes. Later said to be Thomas Lavender's butchers, it was bought in 1874 for £230 by William Rowe, who in turn sold it for £350 to his son of the same name in 1884. The Rowe family operated a grocers & drapery there through to the early part of the century before Arthur George Burgess, a Romford tobacconist, bought Cosy Corner in 1909 for £650. Often known as 'The Old Butchers Shop', it was usually listed as a confectioners' shop and continued in this trade after its sale in 1921 to William Grove. After only five years Grove leased the premises to Mrs Honor Barry in 1926, before selling to Herbert Finch for £2,250 in 1932. It seems that Herbert Finch, a Romford builder, bought the business for his son Sidney, a Romford tobacconist, who along with his wife ran the confectioner's business through the post-war period before selling to Frederick Brooks of Gidea Park for £4,500 in May 1948. With the well-remembered morning coffee and afternoon teas taken in the open air on the pavement outside, it was a sad day when the building, part of the local scene for over 125 years, was acquired by Hornchurch UDC in January 1956 and finally demolished in January 1957 to make way for road widening and 'improvements' which also finally allowed traffic lights to be erected at this junction, after being promised some twenty years earlier.

Cosy Corner, built in 1831, managed to survive only a few years after this picture was taken in the early 1950s.

8

STATION ROAD AND ITS TRADERS

WEST SIDE

ALTHOUGH THE DEVELOPMENT of Griggs' Edwardian garden suburb had included the building of what was then a substantial selection of shops on the east side of Station Road in the parades between St Lawrence Road and the Station Approach, the development of the western side took place in only a piecemeal fashion over the next thirty years. It was only by the outbreak of war in 1939 that the whole side of the road from the junction with St Mary's Lane up to the railway line formed a virtually continuous series of shops. The completion of the west side of Station Road almost exclusively for retail uses took until the 1950s.

Corner of Station Road and St Mary's Lane

Right through into the late 1930s visitors approaching Upminster's Bell Corner from Corbets Tey could not have failed to notice the fully-grown and fine horse-chestnut trees in the grounds of the house on the corner opposite the churchyard. Perhaps not surprisingly the house was known as the Chestnuts, this corner of St Mary's Lane and Station Road came to be known as Chestnuts Corner, while the garage established here was called Chestnuts Garage. The origins of the Chestnuts Garage date back to around 1890, when William (or Billy) Aggiss, a native of Upminster born in Little Gaynes Lane who had worked as a coachman for Mr Henry Hoslin senior at Hoppey Hall, started business on his own account as a jobmaster from premises behind the Bell Inn, hiring out horses and carts and cabs. Business was varied, carrying goods from Covent Garden, taking people on trips to Southend in open landaus and driving couples to the ball. As trade increased, a larger premises was obtained on the corner of Station Road and Hornchurch Road (later St Mary's Lane) – the land behind two houses known as Locksley Villa and the adjacent Chestnuts.

Although it was William Aggiss who in 1912 introduced one of the first cars into Upminster, a Pannard, it was later said that 'he loathed that new opponent

Jack Carter, driver, Richard Stokes, foreman and William Aggiss *(right)* outside the garage in the 1920s.

of the horse . . . a loathing he never lost, even though his garage is one of the largest in the area . . . he kept horses for hire until after the [First] World War ended'. Billy's son Henry James Aggiss (1883-1950) trained originally as a butcher but after the First World War invested his demobilisation money into an old Thorneycroft truck, which allowed the business to expand. The range of services covered not only haulage but removals, a chauffeur's service and a hearse. In later years motor engineering and the sale of petrol was added to the range of services, before a motorcar showroom replaced the former stables and the haulage work was discontinued. The Chestnuts and the adjacent Locksley Villa were sold for development in 1935, and demolished in November 1937, making way for the Burton's tailors' store (Nos. 131 to 133 St Mary's lane).

In time this corner came to be known as Burton's Corner. Burton's stores met the need at the time for smart men's wear at an affordable price, providing a mid-way approach to bespoke tailoring by having trained staff who took measurements at the point of sale with garments mass-manufactured in their north of England factory. Their stores throughout outer London were designed to dominate corner sites such as this, the store in Hornchurch at the junction of High Street and North Street being a fine surviving example.

Following the sale of the corner site to Burton's, Aggiss's built a new work-shop and service bay to cater for the increasing motor trade, with a matched decline in the dominance of their haulage business. The cars sold by Aggiss were usually Austins, which were collected from the factory near Birmingham. This required a journey by the 8am train from Euston, and driving the new vehicle back to Upminster that afternoon. While Henry Aggiss was on such a trip in 1939 his father William, who at the age of eighty-five still kept an active daily involvement in the business, was taken ill, dying in his sleep that night.

After the death of Henry Aggiss in 1950 aged sixty-seven his two sons, George and James, successfully carried on the business until their retirement in 1980 when the Chestnuts Garage ceased trading, to be superseded in turn by Pit Stop Auto Services Ltd., Superdrive Motor Centres Ltd. and currently by Time Tees Cars. This latter business was established under the control of Wally Howes and George Chick, formerly of Vasil Motors, Corbets Tey, who have since updated the service bay and equipment and enlarged the showroom.

Nos. 13 to 19 Station Road

Between the Chestnuts Garage and the former British School, was a terrace of three cottages fronting onto Station Road. Also at No. 13 there was a greengrocers' shed-shop used by Jack Knight of Sullens Farm as an alternative outlet for his market-garden produce (a later Knight's shop was at 7 Byron Parade, Corbets Tey Road).

The first of the terrace (No. 17) was converted to form Sidney Abraham's bakers' shop, the entrance being to the side; at the rear was a detached bake-house built around 1802. Sidney Abraham was one of the brothers of Thomas, Alfred and Clement Abraham, owners of the windmill, and naturally his bread was freshly made with flour ground at his brothers' windmill. It appears that the bakery came into the Abraham's family following Sidney's marriage in 1895 to Florence Hitch, who had inherited the bakery on the death in 1888 of her father Edward Hitch, baker. It remained in the Abraham's ownership until it was sold by auction in March 1952, following Sidney Abraham's death the previous year.

The centre cottage (No. 19) remained a private house, while the cottage at the northern end (No. 21) was John Cant's boot & shoe repair business. When the site of Nos. 15 to 19 Station Road was offered for sale in 1952 Hornchurch UDC acquired the whole site, together with the land to the rear of the Abraham's bakery, in order to provide a much needed car park in central Upminster; further land fronting Gaynes Road was added to provide access to the parking area. This left the full frontage of the site on Station Road available to be commercially developed – the outcome was Essex House with five shops and two floors of office accommodation above. The offices were used from the outset by Ford Motor Company but in later years became surplus to requirements with the

Abraham's bakers and Cant's boot repair premises and a passing 'stop-me-and-buy-one' ice-cream sales man!

setting up of their large administrative offices at Warley. The upper floors of Essex House were then divided into small office units. The current shops in this block (13-19A) are La Grolla, Italian restaurant, The Beauty Rooms, hairdressing and beauty salon, the Lambeth Building Society, the Children's Society charity shop and the Victoria Wine Company, acquired from Augustus Barnett.

NOS. 21-29 STATION ROAD

The site of the former British School, built in 1850/51 and demolished in 1938, is now occupied by four shops, Nos. 21 to 27 Station Road, each with two floors of living accommodation above. This block, which extends to the boundary with Barclays Bank, seems to have been built in 1938 immediately after the school was demolished. The Barclays Bank building (No. 29 Station Road) on the corner of Gaynes Road was originally single storey, probably built around 1926, with the first floor addition dating from the post-war period. The front forecourt is remembered as formerly being a well-cut grassed area in keeping with the village scene, surrounded by white-painted wooden posts connected by a link chain.

NOS. 31 TO 39 STATION ROAD

Now Trinity United Reform church, formerly the Congregational church, opened 1911, and Roope Hall opened in the late 1940s.

ROOMES STORES, NOS. 41 TO 45 STATION ROAD

Not only are Roomes Stores a well-known landmark in central Upminster but the store's history is also closely linked with the development of Upminster itself. James and Sophia Roome and their family were among the first to move to the Edwardian garden suburb in 1908, taking residence at the newly built 16 Engayne Gardens. James was a master draper who, twenty years earlier in 1888, had set up a drapery store, or 'fancy drapers' as it then was, on the west side of Green Street between Plashet Road and Harold Road, in Upton Park, which was then being expanded. Originally described as Royal Terrace, and later 66 Green Street, after renumbering the store's address stabilised in the early years of the century as 366 to 370 Green Street. James Roome, who was born at St Pancras, Middlesex in December 1850, the son of Benjamin and Martha Roome, married Sophia Culpin and the couple lived originally in Fulham, where their older children were born.

The house move to the fashionable Upminster in 1908 was a mark of James Roome's rising status. His new hometown, however, was soon to be his last resting place for in March 1913 he unexpectedly died of heart failure aged sixty-two. His son, M.B. Roome – Millice Benjamin, known as 'Mill' who had joined him when the business became James Roome & Son in 1906 – now assumed full command. It was during Mill Roome's stewardship of the firm

James and Sophia Roome with their children Miss Annie Bertha *(left)*, Millice Benjamin *(centre)*, Miss Ethel Mary *(right)* and Frank A *(front)* in about 1900.

The first Roomes Upminster Store pictured about 1930, after enlargement.

that the major expansion came about. Initially Mill and his sister Annie Bertha Roome continued to develop the Upton Park store but, with the continued housing development of Upminster and the family's connections with the village, it is not surprising that when a 40ft site in Station Road, Upminster became available in 1926, it should be viewed as a perfect location on which to develop. A company, Roomes Stores Ltd., was formed with the financial backing of Mr W.D. Key and Mr F.W. Norledge, and the Station Road site was acquired. Roomes Upminster drapery store opened in 1927 with a staff of around fifteen, and in 1930 the store was enlarged when a further 25ft in Station Road was added and a ground floor extension was built, allowing a furnishing department to be opened.

The development of the Gaynes estate from 1930 further boosted Upminster's population. Roomes acquired further adjacent land in 1934 and plans were developed to concentrate all the company's efforts at Upminster. The transfer of the neon sign from the Upton Park store to Upminster in December 1934 was perhaps a symbolic recognition that Upminster was now the firm's dominant outlet. Just over a year later, in early January 1936, Roomes' Upton Park store was closed, by which time preparations for the rebuilding of the Upminster Station Road store were underway. The new store involved a significant expansion and the design took in the adjacent shops of Lush & Cooks, dyers and dry-cleaners and the hairdressing business of Harold Mobbs (formerly Austin Reynolds), which continued as a kind of 'store within a store'. The department store itself, which opened on 4 May 1937, now boasted a restaurant and many new departments. Sadly, Sophia Roome did not live to see the store's completion, dying aged eighty in August 1936.

The doctor's house and surgery known as Parkway belonging to Dr John Bletsoe was built at the northern junction of Branfill Road and Satation Road (No. 51 Station Road) in 1908 and seems to have been occupied by Dr Bletsoe from the outset. He was joined around the First World War by Dr Arthur Sanderson, forming the partnership of Bletsoe and Sanderson. By the early 1920s this partnership had been replaced by that of Bletsoe, Robinson and Nichols, with Drs Harold Shillito Robinson and Henry Wilfred Lee Nichols covering Emerson Park and Hornchurch respectively, while Dr Bletsoe concentrated on the Upminster end of the large practice. Following the departure of Dr Robinson, Dr Cecil Symons joined the firm in the early 1930s, with his surgery at No.16 Hall Lane at its junction with Deyncourt Gardens.

On the retirement of Dr Bletsoe in March 1939, after thirty years of medical service to Upminster, the doctor's house on the corner of Branfill Road was bought by Roome, the doctor's surgery transferring to Hall Lane under Dr Hill. But the onset of war meant that any plans by Roome to develop the site had to be put on hold. Meanwhile, the third generation of the Roome family, John and David, joined the firm. John entered the business upon leaving school in 1941, after his poor hearing ruled him out from military service, and his brother David joined him in 1946, upon demobilisation. Further land in Branfill Road adjacent to the doctor's house was added in 1955, allowing Roomes' plans to build on the corner of Branfill and Station Road to go ahead. Roomes' furnishing store opened the following year and a top floor was added in 1958.

Throughout this time the Westminster Bank building (No. 49 Station Road) had operated on the other corner of Branfill Road, next to the main Roomes Store. The bank site was bought in 1906 from the Branfill Park Estate by London & City Banking Co. Ltd. and the bank had been built in 1911, originally as the London, County and Westminster Bank, becoming the Westminster Bank in the early 1920s. This situation, with the survival of the bank preventing the two Roomes buildings north and south of Branfill Road forming a logical sequence, was clearly unsatisfactory. But the opportunity to change the situation came only in 1967 when the demolition of the National School building on the opposite side of Station Road provided the chance for Roome to acquire the former school site and strike a land-transfer deal. This allowed the bank to vacate the premises on the corner of Branfill Road and relocate to a newly erected bank building on the other side of the road (8 Station Road). The old Westminster Bank building was adapted as a bookshop by Roome from 1967 until 1972 when it was demolished and a ground

Station Road looking south *c.* 1920. Dr Bletsoe's house and the Westminster Bank building are on the right.

floor only extension of Roomes, accommodating the leather, stationery and book departments, with access to the main store, went ahead. In May 1989 this extension along Branfill Road was totally demolished and the whole site excavated to the level of the main store; a new three-storey air-conditioned building on piled foundations was built, with free access throughout the combined building. This project, completed in October 1990 and probably the largest and most complex commercial development in Upminster for many years, has been successfully trading ever since.

Roomes remains a family business. Although David Roome, who had been joint managing director, retired in 1977, his joint director brother John continues an active interest and his sons Stephen and Michael are the fourth generation of the family to manage the business.

NOS. 53 TO 61 STATION ROAD

Immediately north of the doctor's house was Reginald H. Kemp's chemist's, optician's and chiropody business, established in 1926 (No. 32 Station Road). Bought by Roomes in October 1945, this subsequently accommodated their china department until 1955, when the small shop was demolished, along with the doctor's house next door, to make way for Roomes furnishing store.

Reginald Kemp was the son of Frank Kemp, dairyman, who around the end of the First World War had his Crumpled Horn Dairy at No. 50 Station Road, (now the Wimpy Bar). With the development of the west side of Station

Road, by 1923 Kemp had transferred his dairy business and associated tea-rooms across the road to the enlarged premises at No. 55. Milk was sold from the dairy shop where a milk churn was kept in a water-filled concrete basin – an attempt at refrigeration. Milk was served by a dipper from the churn into customers' jugs, which then had to be carried home without spilling it. In the summer ice-cream was served in the tearoom in the cellar, illuminated by daylight from the laylight in the pavement outside (this can still be seen outside Daniel Ray's studio).

Clifford Buttle succeeded Kemp in the dairy trade in the mid-1930s and, after a long battle to establish a Crown Post Office in Upminster through the late 1930s, the dairy site was converted to this use. The post office remained at this location until its transfer in recent years to the agency office in Martin McColl's newsagents at No. 24. Daniel Ray photographic studios now occupy the former dairy and post office premises (now Nos. 55 & 57).

Further north was a pair of semi-detached houses built by W.P. Griggs and Co. and closely associated with that company. The southernmost, then No. 57 (but now No. 61 Baccarat), was the private house of Joseph Gillings and family, one of the main contractors used by Griggs, while the adjoining semi (Nos. 59 – now 63) housed the estate office from which W.P. Griggs & Co. and their successors, Upminster Estates Ltd., marketed their housing developments at Upminster Garden Suburb. This was rented by Roomes Stores on a twenty-one year lease from August 1935 and used as a menswear shop. This now houses the Essex Joinery shop. Upminster Estates relocated their estate office to what is now No. 59, a small half-unit bridging the gap between former Nos. 55 and 57. Until a few years ago this housed Beresfords, successor to Upminster Estates, and now accommodated CISS Financial Services.

On the railway side to this house there was a single storey extension, originally also part of the estate office. From the mid-1930s this appears to have become No. 61 from which Doris Boyle ran her ladies hairdresser's business (now 65 Floral Affairs). From the same period for many years Cakebread Robey & Co., operated a builder's merchants business in the house and the land adjoining. From 1941 to 1944 this was used by 'E' company 4th Essex Home Guard as their quartermaster's stores.

9

CHURCH AND CHAPEL
RELIGIOUS LIFE IN UPMINSTER

WOULD UPMINSTER'S BEST-KNOWN clergyman William Derham, rector from 1689 to 1735, recognise St Laurence's church if he were to come back today? The answer is probably 'Yes' for although the church has been subjected to several major enlargements and rebuilding over the past two-and-a-half centuries, enough of the appearance of the smaller country parish church survives to provide a visual link to the past. In particular Derham would have little difficulty in recognising the tower with its spire from which he carried out his experiments into natural phenomena, such as measuring the speed of sound, using this elevated platform as his observatory for his views across the Thames valley.

The parish church of St Laurence, standing as it does in a prominent position at the crossroads which marked the original village centre, has a long history and tradition at the heart of parish life. The name Upminster may indicate that the parish was host to a 'mother' church (or minster) which served the surrounding area in Saxon times. 'Minsters' were often regarded as superior churches as they were often long-established, and many had been founded in or before the eighth century to assist in the process of conversion of the area. This fits with the tradition that the 'Up-minster' was one of five minsters or mission centres established in Essex in the middle of the seventh century by St Cedd (or Chad), a Celtic priest sent into Essex on foot by Finan, Bishop of Lindisfarne, along with a companion priest to spread the gospel. The other four minsters are said to be Bradwell-on-Sea, Tilbury, Southminster, and Canewdon, although only Cedd's foundation of the Bradwell and Tilbury churches can be regarded as definitive.

Irrespective of whether Cedd was involved the original church at Upminster would have been small in size and, in the absence of local building stone, would have been built using the only readily available material, timber and thatch. The uncommon dedication to St Laurence, which is shared by only a small number of churches in England and Wales, also suggests an early origin. In Europe, for

St Laurence's church, 1793.

instance, it became a common dedication for churches after Otto the Great's victory over the Magyars on St Laurence's Day in 955. St Laurence was a Christian martyr of the third century who was said to have met his death in 258 by roasting on a grid-iron over a slow fire – hence the grid-iron symbol with which be became associated. He was one of seven deacons of Rome who by tradition when asked by the Prefect of Rome to deliver up the treasure of his church assembled hundreds of poor saying 'These are the treasures of the church'. He became one of the most famous saints of the Roman church, whose feast day is celebrated on 10 August.

No trace of Upminster's original church remains. At sometime during the reign of King John (1199-1216) the church was rebuilt in stone. The only survivals are the lower stages of the present tower, parts of the massive wooden framing which supports the shingled and leaded spire. Early in the fourteenth century the church was enlarged by the addition of the North Aisle and one ancient feature from this building which has escaped destruction is the arcade separating the nave and north aisle. The original chapel of Gaynes or St Mary's at the east end of the church also dates from this century. The chapel with its interesting scries of mainly Tudor wall-mounted brasses and some memorials to the Branfill family of Upminster Hall and their relations is one of the most interesting features of the church. Rebuilt by Sir James Esdaile of New Place in 1771, the chapel's rights apparently belonged to and descended with that manor: it contained a large family pew for the use of the occupiers of New

Place, as well as six other pews which were often rented out to other families. Esdaile was also responsible for much restoration work to the church.

On 15 March 1861 a public meeting was held in the National School in response to the offer of the ageing Rector John Rose Holden to contribute £1,000 towards the enlargement of the church. A committee was set up to raise subscriptions, to which the curate Francis Sterry donated £50. The architect Mr William Gibbs Bartleet of South Weald, who later designed Hill Place, was invited to submit a design for a 'thorough reparation of the church, and the providing of additional accommodation for 150 sittings and the building of a new vestry'. The lowest quotation came from a Mr Burrell of Norwich whose tender of £1,362 12s won him the job. From June 1861 the rectory barn was prepared and afterwards used for Divine Worship, while work took place over the rest of that year and into 1862. Work was completed in February 1862 and the church reopened for worship on 1 March.

The church had almost been completely remodelled in a style which closely reproduced the style of its predecessor. However, sadly in the process many things of historic interest – numerous effigies, coats of arms and inscriptions on the floor – were discarded. The screen of St Mary's chapel was thrown out and lay in a ditch for a year before it was rescued, renovated and put back in the church. The chancel, north aisle, St Mary's chapel and south porch had almost been completely rebuilt, while the tower was repaired and its covering of ivy removed, the latter at an additional cost of £90.

The parish church *c.* 1911. The growing population was already putting pressure on accommodation.

In the early years of this century after two decades of population growth which followed the building of the garden suburb, St Laurence church became inadequate for its growing congregation. In May 1928, following fund-raising efforts, the essential work of enlarging the church began, carried out by Messrs William Bell and Son of Saffron Walden, to the designs of Sir Charles Nicholson. It now seems strange that on 2 July 1928 the foundation stone was laid with full Masonic Ceremonial by the Worshipful Brother J.H. Salter, JP DL, Deputy Grand Master. The extensions, which cost around £7,000 with an additional £750 spent on improving the organ, almost doubled the area of the old church. The chancel was removed and the present choir and sanctuary built at the east end, while on the south side the choir and St George's chapel were added, as was the Lady chapel at the end of the north aisle. The dedication ceremony for the enlarged church was performed by the Bishop of Chelmsford in October 1929.

The church is sited on land which adjoined the Manor of Gaynes, although almost certainly the location of the church predated the establishment of either Gaynes or Upminster Hall Manors, in the south and north of the parish. From the early thirteenth century there was no formal link between the ownership of either manor and the patronage of the living which passed through a number of hands before it was bought by William Holden of Birmingham in 1780, in which family it remained for almost 200 years.

William Derham DD, Rector of Upminster, 1685–1736.

Upminster's most famous incumbent was William Derham, DD – rector from 1689 until his death in 1735. Unlike many of his predecessors and successors who lived elsewhere and employed curates to look after the parish, Derham lived in Upminster, choosing High House opposite the church as his residence due to the dilapidated state of the rectory. Possibly the poor state of the rectory at that time was due to previous rectors' non-residence. According to Wilson, Dr Derham was 'pretty tall and seemed to be of a strong and healthy constitution, His moral character was quite amiable'. However, despite his wisdom and learning he was no preacher. A graduate of Oxford University he had been vicar of Wargrave, Berkshire for seven years before being presented to the living at Upminster. He took a particular interest in the study of nature, mathematics and philosophy and soon was chosen Fellow of the Royal Society. He came to the notice of the then Prince of Wales, later George II, who made him his Chaplain, and in 1716 he was installed as Canon of Windsor, after which he spent less time at Upminster. He did, however, die at High House and was buried in the chancel of the parish church, although there is no memorial to him.

An understanding of the religious history of Upminster over the past two centuries goes some way to explaining many developments in the parish, for the village was split into two main camps: those supporters of the established church who worshipped at the parish church of St Laurence and those who preferred the nonconformist method of worship, most of whom attended the Congregational church. The first signs of nonconformity were already evident in the parish before Derham's incumbency. In 1672 the house of Samuel Springham in the north part of Upminster was licensed as a Presbyterian Meeting House, and this congregation still existed in 1708. But it was the events of almost a century later that led to a more permanent nonconformist gathering.

John Rose Holden was presented as the rector of Upminster in 1780 by his father William Holden of Birmingham who had bought the patronage. It was J.R. Holden and his son of the same name who succeeded him in 1799 who alienated many parishioners by engaging in a dispute over tithes. By ancient right the clergy were entitled to one-tenth of all produce of the parish (the tithe) but over time the practice changed from supplying the rector with produce to making a fixed money payment – this had been the case for some years in Upminster before Holden took the living. However, the closing years of the eighteenth century were times of rising inflation and the rector found that his income was getting less and less in real terms with no increase in tithe payments. On 30 May 1798 J.R. Holden senior gave notice to the parishioners that from the following 8 May 1799 he proposed to take his tithe in kind, or alternatively required a cash payment of 6s an acre. This was met with considerable ill-feeling locally, so much so that on the day that the new arrangement was due to come into force Holden resigned his living, to be succeeded by his son who took up the gauntlet. For two years J.R. Holden junior struggled to put this change into effect, tramping the length and breadth of the parish noting how many cattle, sheep and lambs each farmer had, estimating how much tithe was due to him, and even grabbing the produce – hay, wool, ducks, chickens and eggs etc – that he believed were due. Not surprisingly the situation got worse and the young rector was met by verbal and physical violence by some farmers. Holden leased the tithe to Mr William Edwards for £700 and it was now Edwards and his men who had to enforce the collection of the tithes. Although the parishioners wanted a peaceful outcome to the dispute, after Edwards' involvement they felt they had to fight on. But Edwards had no more success than the rector in gathering the produce and took Holden to court because he could not collect the full value of his lease from the parish. It was many years before the strong feelings generated by this bitter dispute died down and the situation was only settled once and for all in 1842 when the rector's tithe was assessed at £1,052 under the Tithe Commutation Act.

The old congregational chapel on Upminster Hill, opened for worship in 1800.

The registering of William Nokes' house at Bridge Farm for independent worship on 1 October 1799 was a direct consequence of this falling out between the Holdens and a group of prominent parishioners. The next year James Nokes of Hunts Farm and others built a permanent Congregational chapel on the present site on Upminster Hill on land which had formed part of the manor of Gaynes. Almost half the cost of £486 was raised by subscription and the balance was met by three friends who provided the money on loan. The chapel opened for worship on 8 June 1800 and the following year a 'Church of Protestant Dissenters' was formed when six members signed a covenant. One of the original benefactors, Mrs Elizabeth Fries who died in 1807, left a bequest of the interest on £100 stock towards the maintenance of the chapel.

The freehold of the chapel was bought for £28 in 1802 and in 1819 a plot of land to the south was acquired and the chapel enlarged and a vestry added. A new brick front was added in 1847 when repairs were also carried out, and in 1873 there was a complete renovation which included new pews to replace the high-backed originals which made it difficult for the preacher to see his congregation. During the twelve weeks that the works were under way by Wilson (Upminster's historian) and Martin, services were held in the British School Room. The refurbished church was opened on 20 September 1873.

The behaviour of Upminster's third rector from the Holden family, Philip Melancthon Holden, who took over on the death of his long-serving uncle John Rose Holden junior in 1862, did nothing to heal the rift between the Congregationalists and followers of the established Church. Popular at first the new rector fell out with his parishioners in 1873 after he had a liaison with, then married, a parishioner leading to his suspension for two years, and for many years following he was involved in several disputes. The rector's disgrace coincided with the rise of the Congregationalists, with many leading parishioners to the fore. Among them was Henry Joslin of Gaynes who in 1865 had married the widow of Rev. George Clayton, a prominent nonconformist preacher, while in Joslin's brother-in-law Alfred Morgan Carter, who took over as minister in 1879, the congregational church found a popular figurehead. Although just twenty-four years old on taking up the ministry fresh from theological college, the Hackney-born Carter soon gained the friendship of Upminster folk by systematically visiting the people of the district. He lived in the Manse, which on his arrival was a house adjoining the chapel, which was demolished in 1872 to allow the westerly extension of Hill Place. In exchange for this the owner Temple Soanes Esq. gave the church a piece of land on the opposite side of the road on which a much larger and more comfortable Manse was built.

Carter's popular ministry had a sad end. In 1900 while out walking in a field at North Ockendon, while inspecting a possible site for a new cemetery for the parish, the reverend twisted his leg, badly injuring his kneecap. He never fully recovered from this injury and the next year had to have his leg amputated. In considerable pain, which seriously hampered his pastoral and ministerial duties, the Rev. Carter made the decision to retire in 1907 when his eyesight too began to fail. He died in 1916.

Until a new minister could be found the vacant ministry was guided by three deacons – Henry Joslin, Alfred Abraham and Humphrey Vellacott. The latter was a devout Devonian who had come to Essex in 1878, originally farming at Tyrrell's Hall in Little Thurrock before moving to Upminster in 1898. This period without a minister coincided with a difficult period for the church as the Upminster Garden Suburb's rapid expansion brought with it an influx of new worshippers from other districts. Carter's successor the Rev. Stanley Bloomfield was ordained at the church in October 1909 and within a few

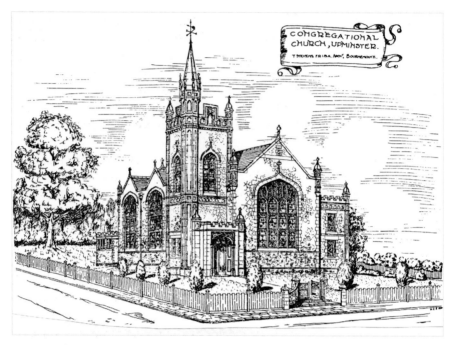

Architect's design of the proposed congregational church – the planned tower and steeple were not finally built.

months some forty-four new members were formally enrolled into the church. The Rev. Bloomfield's local connections were strengthened in March 1911 when he married Miss Maud Joslin, daughter of Walter Joslin of Hunts.

With the establishment of the new minister, plans which had been drawn up for the building of a new Congregational church could now be put into effect. Very generous donations soon amounted to over £2,000, with a bazaar in the grounds of Henry Joslin's Gaynes Park alone raising £150 towards the building fund. A further £400 was raised by the sale to the Plymouth Brethren of the old chapel on Upminster Hill. With other fund-raising some £2,800 of the total of £4,000 was obtained, leaving the balance to be met by a series of loans, interest-free, for ten years. On 29 March 1911 the new church on the corner of Station Road and Gaynes Road was opened, just eighteen months after the scheme was launched.

Additions to the premises came in 1923 opening of the Commemoration and Minor Halls, erected by W.P. Griggs & Co. at a cost of £2,300. Lady Griggs laid the foundation stone in February 1923 and the halls were formally opened three months later. At the same time Lady Griggs presented the stained glass window at the back of the church in memory of her late husband, Sir Peter. Plans to build another hall on land north of the church, close to Roomes, were first mooted around 1935 but in the absence of an early decision to proceed these ideas were delayed by the outbreak of war. The Commemoration Hall had been requisitioned for use by the Civil Defence during the war years and at the end of hostilities it was returned to the church, together with a payment of £1,600 towards restoration and repair. The continued growth in Sunday school attendance and the lack of accommodation for various organisations led to the decision to build the long-awaited hall. This was built in 1947 and later named in honour of Rev. Robert Roope, the church's minister from 1940 to 1951.

The Wesleyan Methodist church in Upminster cannot claim a long history or trace its growth to any local conflict of interest. In fact it only came into being in 1910 as an offshoot of the Seven Kings church, part of the Ilford Circuit. In 1909 two society classes attached to that church decided to hold a picnic and chose Upminster as their venue. They were greatly impressed with the area, no doubt not only influenced by the continuing local beauty but by the possibilities which were offered by the rapidly developing garden suburb. Steps were put in hand to form a church in Upminster and a site in Hall Lane with a frontage of 100 feet and a depth of 295 feet was bought from W.P. Griggs for £700 in June 1910. When a permanent church was built at Seven Kings to house their growing numbers the iron church it replaced was re-erected on the newly acquired Upminster site in July 1910. As the Upminster Methodist community grew it was likewise decided to invest in a permanent church to replace the iron structure which 'although neat enough in appearance . . . seemed incongruous amid its ultra-modern surroundings'. A building fund was

Upminster's Methodist Church opened in 1923, replacing a temporary 'tin tabernacle'.

begun in 1920, and by the end of 1921 £367 had been raised. Work on a new church was started late in 1922 by W.P. Griggs & Co. to plans by Gunton & Gunton. On 23 February 1923 a stone-laying ceremony was performed with Lady Griggs laying the first stone, followed by other dignitaries with scholars from the Sunday school also each taking a turn to lay a brick. By that time the fund had risen to around £2,100 and promise of help brought the sum to £4,600, still some £3,000 short of the total project cost of £7.600. With the opening of the new premises the 'Tin Tabernacle', which had already served two church communities, continued in use as a church hall at the rear.

Upminster's Roman Catholic community also worshipped in a temporary building until the later erection of a permanent church. In 1922 with Griggs & Co.'s development of the New Place Estate south of St Mary's Lane a site became available which was bought by the Catholic Diocese of Brentwood. Building plans for a church of 'absolute simplicity and utility' with accommodation for 400 were approved in July 1922, and G Makings, contractors of Romford, soon started work on what was viewed from the outset as a temporary church; a nearby house became the Presbytery. In just six months the work was complete and on 25 January 1925 Dr Doubleday, Bishop of Brentwood, opened and consecrated the church dedicated to St Joseph, which was initially part of the parish of Romford. Father Michael Healy, curate to Father Julius Van Meenan of Romford, served the small Upminster Catholic community and Fr. Healy was appointed parish priest in October 1923 when

Upminster's original Catholic church opened in 1922 near the junction of St Mary's Lane and Sunnyside Gardens.

Upminster became a separate parish. Upminster's Catholic community was strengthened in May 1927 when a small group of nuns, the order of the Institute of the Religious of the Sacred Heart of Mary, bought the Hill Place Estate from Dr Storrs Brookfield and established a convent and private boarding and day school there.

It was soon evident that the church site on the corner of Sunnyside Gardens lacked the potential to be developed further in line with Upminster's rapid population growth. When serious faults in the fabric of the building came to light it was realised that another site would have to be found to cater for the village's catholic community. The Sunnyside Gardens site was sold for £1,000 to the post office for the building of a telephone exchange and site on the corner of St Mary's Lane and Champion Road, part of the Mavisbank Estate, was bought. The church's purchase included the surviving property of Mavisbank itself, built in 1850 by Thomas Turner, a cattle salesman (after whom it was known locally as 'Hoof Hall'), which was pressed into service as the Presbytery.

On 3 December 1932, Bishop Doubleday opened a temporary church in a wooden building, which had possibly once served as an army billet, located to the north of the present church on the site of the current Presbytery. After years of fund-raising, by the summer of 1938 the bishop gave the go ahead for work to build the new Upminster church, for which £5,000 had been raised of the estimated cost of £8,000. The plans were approved in December 1938, and in February 1939 work began on the neo-Gothic replacement, designed by Marshall and Archard, architects of London. After a month of favourable weather conditions allowed work to proceed well, the ceremony for laying and blessing of the foundation stone was held on 25 March 1938. Just seven months later on 28 October 1939, seven weeks after war was declared, the newly completed church of St Joseph was opened by Bishop Doubleday.

The Baptists were the final religious congregation to establish a base in Upminster when the church began in 1934 with thirty-three members, with the support of the North Street Baptist church, Hornchurch. A Sunday school and chapel were rapidly built between July and November 1935 at a cost of £3,000 in Springfield Gardens, although the present church was not built until 1959.

10
SLATES, STROKES
AND POT-HOOKS
UPMINSTER SCHOOLDAYS

THE PASSING OF the 1870 Education Act, which the Essex historian Dr Harold Priestley described as 'one of the greatest steps forward in the social evolution of England', had a major effect in many English parishes. For the first time the government of England could step in to make sure that enough school places were available to cater for the children of the 'labouring classes'. But by the time the Act appeared, Upminster had already been served by two schools for almost twenty years.

It was in 1851 – the year of the Great Exhibition – that these two Upminster schools opened. On 28 February that year the British School, run by the nonconformists under the influence of the British and Foreign Bible School Society, opened on what is now the site next to Barclays Bank near the corner of Gaynes and Station Roads. Then just a month later on 25 March 1851 came the opening of the National School, so-called because education was provided under the scheme of the 'National Society for Promoting the Education of the Poor in the Principles of the Established Church'. This school and the adjoining master's house were sited where the National Westminster Bank now stands in Station Road.

Upminster was not alone in Essex in having separate 'church and chapel' schools. But this arrangement was hardly surprising in Upminster considering the fragile relations between the Anglican rector and the by now well-established local non-conformist congregation. The rector gave his patronage and support to the National School while the minister of the Congregational chapel took a necessarily close interest in the British School. For nineteen years each co-existed but remained virtually separate, and the siting of the schools, more or less facing each other across opposite sides of what is now Station Road, almost seemed to suggest open competition for the right to instruct the children of the parish.

The British School, with its 'spacious, airy and light' schoolroom which was 'considered large enough for the requirements of 150 children', was built by

Upminster's British School, opened on 28 February 1851.

the local builder William Hook on land given by Edward Dawson of Aldcliff Hall, Lancaster. A significant proportion of the building costs were subscribed by Mr Thomas Johnson of Gaynes Villa, and fittingly the first stone was laid by Mrs Johnson, daughter of the late Rev. Clayton, on 26 September 1850. The school opened for pupils just five months later under Miss Elizabeth Treble, the first mistress who was paid an annual salary of £40. Places were funded by subscriptions and 'school pence'.

The site for the National School was presented by Mrs Branfill of Upminster Hall. Work started a little earlier than at the British School opposite, but the schoolroom and adjoining master's house opened one month later than its competitor, on 25 March 1851. Thirty years later Wilson described the buildings as 'in the Tudor style, built of red brick with white dressings, &c., the copings and ornamental parts being of Caen stone. At the north-west angle, upon an open bell tower, a slated spire rises to the height of about fifty feet.' Supposedly built for 100 children, in Wilson's not unbiased opinion, the schoolroom was 'somewhat restricted and inconvenient in shape' and could 'scarcely accommodate conveniently more than 80 children'. The first master was Thomas Eastgate, a forty-one-year-old born in Ashford, Middlesex, who lived in the adjacent schoolhouse with his wife Helen.

Earlier nonconformist schools can be dated to at least 1800/1 when a master from Thomas Talbot's private school taught at Sunday school in the then-new Congregational chapel on Upminster Hill; later in 1833 there is reference to two Sunday schools supported by the Independents. The National School had been preceded by a church day- and Sunday school, supported by subscription. In 1846/47 there were reported to be sixty-two pupils taught in a schoolroom, with a master and two mistresses; there was also a teacher's house.

The 1870 Education Act made limited obvious difference, except that the schools for the first time were subject to an annual visit by one of Her Majesties Inspectors, appointed by the Board of Education. The master of the National School, Mr Bowden, and the mistress of the British School, Miss Mary Emma Heath, were required to submit themselves for certification under the Act. In May 1871, for instance, the inspector considered Miss Heath's instruction 'to be satisfactory', although the number of pupils – over fifty of all ages – were considered 'in excess of the teaching power', making it difficult for her to keep order. The situation was only partly remedied the following year when she received the help of a pupil-teacher. Pupil-teachers were an important part of the teaching strength, serving under the certificated teacher for up to thirty hours weekly during normal school hours and receiving as well an hour's instruction from the headteacher either before or after school. Martha Tween, the British School's first pupil-teacher, received a salary of £10, increasing by £2 10s per year.

Pupil numbers at both schools continued to rise. By 1880 there were 94 children on the books of the National School, although the average attendance was just 57, while at the British School numbers on roll had reached 101, with 67 attending on average. This growth caused pressure both on accommodation and teaching resources. At the British School Miss Heath struggled to keep order alone, supported only by two pupil monitors paid 4s weekly, who the Inspector felt did not render 'assistance of any value', while the pupil-teacher there was dismissed when she had failed her second year examination. An assistant teacher was appointed in July 1882 but by then standards had already fallen too far across the whole range of subjects and year groups, leading to deductions in the grant for 1883. The report of HM Inspector Mr Helps in December 1883 remained critical and recommended that the two schools should be merged:

> The instruction of the Infants must of necessity interfere with that of the elder children . . . In my opinion this school should be conducted as a Girls' and Infants' School, the Boys going to the National School, and the Infants now taught there coming here, and I would strongly advise the Managers to confer with the Managers of the National School as to the feasibility of this amalgamation.

At first both sides were opposed to the merger of their schools and to the setting up of a School Board for the parish which it was felt would add a burden to the rates. A meeting of the parish's ratepayers at the end of May

The spire of the National School was a familiar landmark in the centre of Upminster.

1884 concluded that joint operation of schools under separate committees was the preferred way forward, but the Anglicans seem to have held more objections. The nonconformists had no fear of a school run on non-denominational lines, as the prominent local Congregationalist Henry Joslin stated, 'The Bible should be taught in both schools but no catechism or creed taught'. In June 1884 Rev. Carter, on behalf of the British School Managers, advised the Board of Education that the setting up of a joint School Board was being opposed by the Trustees of the National School who maintained that their Trust Deed prevented this. In frustration the British School Managers announced that they would be unable to carry on after the end of December 1884 unless a School Board was established.

The Board of Education advised the British School Managers that their proposal was not definite enough, so in November 1884 the managers resolved 'that the school should be closed at the end of January 1885' and that it would not be reopened 'as a voluntary school after that date'. The Board's Inspector continued to criticise the arrangements and applied further pressure through reductions in the annual grant indicating at the end of 1884 that the 'filthy condition' of the boys' 'offices' at the British School pointed

> Unmistakably to the need for the Boys being placed under the control of a Master: they would then learn these habits of order and cleanliness which under the Mistress they have not acquired. The management of Boys in these matters is naturally very difficult to a Mistress.

In the face of this pressure, early in 1885 agreement was finally reached for the schools to be placed under the control of the School Board. Despite their opposition, the leading Anglicans, including the lord of the manor of Upminster Hall, Mr Champion Branfill, came forward for election to the Board. Among those who joined him were the Congregational Minister, Rev. Carter and Henry Joslin. A five-member School Board was set up on 30 January 1885 and the schools were finally merged under the control of the newly elected Board on 21 June 1885. The premises remained the property of the British and National School managers, who rented them to the School Board for use for twenty-one years. In September 1885, shortly after the schools restarted after the summer break, thirty-five girls and twenty-five infants were transferred from the National School to the British School, who in return sent thirty boys the other way. This unequal transaction only served to emphasise the shortage of accommodation at the British School, a fact that the annual inspection could not fail to point out. 'A Class-Room properly furnished and supplied with suitable apparatus is required', reported the inspector at the end of 1885, 'also a Cloak-room and Lavatory'. The School Board acted promptly: the British School managers soon agreed their proposal to make the necessary additions, which were eventually completed in 1888, raising the capacity to 190 places, with the infants transferring to the new classroom on 26 April. The National School was rebuilt in 1897, increasing the accommodation to 126 although average attendance in 1899 was still only 74. A former pupil of the British School later described infant school life in the late 1890s:

> We were taught to write on slates, making strokes and pot-hooks; until we could form the letters of the alphabet, and gradually put letters together to form words. There were frames with coloured beads to teach us to count. The teacher had a large frame on wheels to match our small frames . . . We sang action pieces and marched to the music of the harmonium; also to recite nursery rhymes with appropriate action. By the time we were seven years old, we knew our 'twelve times tables', could write and read simple books, do simple arithmetic, plain and purl knitting.

At the British School average attendance at the turn of the century hovered around 120 but many situations arose to prevent it reaching what the head considered acceptable. Many children from the more remote parts of the parish lived several miles away from the school and had little option but to walk there and back, 'the elder children would "pick-a-back" their small brothers and sisters'. (In the 1920s this problem was partly remedied by employing a contractor to convey children from Hacton, Blue Houses and Hunts Hill on Aveley Road by lorry to the school and back each day.)

Class at Upminster's British School in the early years of the 20th century.

The onset of severe weather sometimes meant that all but the most local children stayed away: on 6 November 1899, for instance, less than half the children (just fifty-nine) were present at the Girls and Infants' School 'on account of the rain'. Each summer from late June or early July the advent of the pea-picking season resulted in as many as one quarter of the pupils missing school, while the start of the school year in September was often marred by the absence of many children gleaning after the harvest. Illness and epidemics also took their toll. In January 1902 all children from Hacton hamlet were sent home 'on account of Small Pox being there'; in April 1903 the school reopened after the Easter break only to close for a week as eighty children were absent with measles; in February 1905 the school was closed for ten weeks due to similar outbreak, this time of scarlet fever. The effects of whooping cough, mumps and other ailments also took their toll on attendance levels from time to time.

George Frederick West was the headteacher of the National School and its successor, the Boys' School, for forty-one years. He took over in 1877 when Upminster was still a tiny village with no railway and when he retired in 1918 the first phase of the garden suburb development was almost finished with the next stage due to begin. By the time of his death in January 1932 aged seventy-eight, work on the Gaynes Park Estate was already underway. Although not a local man, born in Wooburn in Buckinghamshire, West played a full part in the life of the community and, as his obituary stated, 'had come to be regarded as an institution'. Said to be 'keenly interested in local government', he was elected to the parish council when it was set up in 1894, and was the first parish clerk for two years, continuing to serve on the council until 1928, holding the role of chairman from 1910-14. After his retirement he retained his interest in education as one of the school's managers. Although West was 'inclined to be reserved', the 'cheery smile and pleasant personality' of this likeable man were much missed in the village, in particular by the generations of schoolchildren who had received their educational grounding in his care. Nearly eighty years after his retirement his memory is cheekily recalled by the following verse:

> Old Daddy West is a very fine man
> He tries to teach you all he can
> Reading, 'Riting, 'Rithmetic
> He doesn't forget to give you the stick

Many of the new inhabitants of Upminster Garden Suburb, particularly those living 'over the bridge', were solidly middle-class families for whom an education for their children at the council school would not have been 'the done thing'. Griggs recognised this from the outset and an early development was the opening on 1 October 1907 of a private preparatory school – Upminster High School – in a house at the junction of Hall Lane and Waldegrave Gardens. The Principal, Miss Emma Browne, BA, gave up her school in Scotland to open the Upminster school which started with twelve pupils and within just over a year had risen to thirty-five, three resident; by 1918 there were seventy pupils there. A former pupil from the late 1920s recalls that Miss Laura, the principal's sister, looked after domestic arrangements, while tuition was provided by the Misses Potter, McPherson and Gillings, the latter the daughter of Mr Gillings of Station Road, who taught music. Miss Browne, who retired as head in about 1929 when she was sixty-four years old, was succeeded by a Miss Parry, but the school failed to live up to its former status and had closed before 1933. At about the age of ten most pupils went on to Palmers College in Grays, in those days a fee-paying institution. Another private school, Upminster College, operated from Deyncourt Gardens in temporary buildings; Miss Elizabeth Currie was listed as the Principal in 1937. In 1926 the school had occupied a house in St Mary's Lane and the Principal had been Miss Olga Cook.

Minster or High House School on the south side of Upminster Hill, which was opened by Miss Renwick in the house next to the chapel in 1915, was a private school with a good reputation. A former pupil from the end of the First World War recalled that the school 'was in a lovely white Georgian house at the top of Upminster Hill. The headmistress was very strict and always wore her hair in a bun, and to me as a child she always seemed very big, but everyone was happy there, and I especially liked the dancing classes.'

Upminster, Hall Lane.

Upminster High School at the junction of Hall Lane and Waldegrave Gardens (now Hurstwood Court).

Under the 1902 Education Act the local School Board ceased to be responsible for the overall control of the council schools, and the Essex County Council became the 'Local Education Authority'. So when the effects of the development of the Upminster garden suburb from 1907 further affected the overcrowding of the Upminster schools, it was the county authority, through their Romford District Sub-Committee, who were required to act. Even in 1904, before the house building had started, the girls' section was said to be 'in poor premises, with old and unsuitable furniture' with the infants were accommodated in 'conditions which render teaching difficult'. However, it was only in December 1911 that the county council took the first tentative steps to address the situation, recommending that the district sub-committee should consider the erection of a new school for girls and infants, planning to leave the Boys' School intact.

During early 1913 the search for a site for the new school was underway in earnest and the County's School Buildings and Supply Committee recommended that 'as the matter was now urgent' their chairman (W.P. Griggs) and the county architect should have power to act as soon as the report of the Romford District was available – the County Education Committee, however, did not accept this recommendation. The district recommended the purchase of a site in May 1913 and an agreement was reached with W. P. Griggs & Co. to buy two and a half acres of the New Place estate with a frontage of 200ft on Cranham Lane at a price of £385 per acre, £963 in all.

In January 1914 perhaps sensing a lack of urgency by the county authorities the Romford District Sub-Committee brought forward proposals 'involving considerable expenditure' to alter the existing buildings. The following month, the Education Committee agreed to issue public notices declaring the council's intention to build a new school for 500 children. Despite the outbreak of war in August 1914 it appeared that the school would go ahead and in February 1915 it was agreed to go ahead with the plans, provided tenders were not sought before January 1916. But, eight months later the Education Committee decided not to invite tenders 'until a date to be fixed'.

In June 1919, soon after hostilities ceased, the Upminster and Cranham Ratepayers Association asked the Board of Education why the Essex County Council had taken no action to build a school on their new site. But what they had not bargained for was that after the war the London County Council would embark on the massive Becontree housing estate, which required a major investment by the county in new schools to serve the rapidly growing population located from London into the former Essex countryside. Despite frequent urging from Upminster's parish council to 'get a move on' it was to be seven further years before the county authorities set plans in hand, during which time the impact of further housing developments on the Upminster Hall and New Place Estates were being felt. The costs of keeping the schools in good repair were also considerable: £250 was spent on 'external and internal repairs' in 1919 and three years later £104 was needed for 'external painting and repairs' and 'repairs to playground'. In July 1926 the Education Committee agreed to seek approval for 'the erection of a school for 350 in the first instance' at an estimated cost of

Class at Upminster School ('The Bell') in the late 1920s, with Mr Cox, Headmaster.

£12,420. The Board of Education judged that the public notices issued in 1914 had lapsed so in September 1926 fresh notices about the proposed new school had to be published in the *Essex Times*. By November 1926 the situation was severe: it was stated that fifty children in Upminster were known to be awaiting admission and the school managers felt they appeared 'to be a laughing stock'. Recognising the increasingly serious situation, in September 1926 the county council sought and received approval to provide Upminster with a temporary portable building to accommodate 150 pupils in three classrooms at a cost of £950 while the permanent buildings were being erected.

Children from the infants' school finally transferred to their new temporary surroundings on 1 April 1927 and a year later at the end of April 1928 came the opening of the permanent building, costing over £10,500 and with furniture costs of £450. The new school, officially Upminster Council School but from the outset better known as 'The Bell School' due to its location next to the inn of the same name, comprised six classrooms, each accommodating fifty children, and a central hall, for temporary use as two classrooms. Mr F.J. Cox, headmaster of the old Boys' School, was appointed headmaster of the new school which catered for the older children up to the school leaving age of fourteen, with Miss M. Jackman, headmistress of the old Girls' & Infants' School, taking over as head of the junior department (i.e. the younger children rather than what is now regarded as junior). As the number of children still continued to rise rapidly the portable building continued to be needed for use as the infants' department, and an additional room had to be taken over from the 'senior department'. The now-vacated British School building was kept in use as a cookery facility; before that for many years the older girls had to go to Mawney Road School in Romford for such lessons. The National School was similarly kept in use but as a woodwork and practical instruction centre for boys.

Another addition to Upminster's educational facilities came in May 1927 when the Roman Catholic nuns of the Institute of the Religious of the Sacred Heart of Mary bought Hill Place and established their convent and private boarding and day school – The Convent Collegiate School – in St Mary's Lane. Rev. Mother Leonard was the first headmistress of this school, which initially catered for girls of all ages and boys up to the age of eight. New school buildings were planned in 1930, but had still not been completed when war broke out; a Georgian-style red brick chapel was built against the east end of Hill Place in 1935, but this had to be demolished in the 1960s due to structural problems following subsidence. During the war the school was evacuated complete to Chilton House in Buckinghamshire, reopening in Upminster in September 1946. As a result of the major changes which followed the 1944 Education Act, the school ceased to be a private boarding school at the end of the summer term 1949, after which it was granted voluntary aided status receiving funding from Essex County Council as the education authority.

The former residence of Hill Place became a convent and school in 1927.

The parish council pressed for the completion of 'The Bell School' to its planned 700 places and in March 1930 the county council came forward with plans to complete the school in 1931/32, receiving approval from the Board of Education in January 1931. Further land was needed, however, and, after negotiations with Gates & Son the owner's agent, the council agreed to buy part of the adjacent lands of High House at a cost of £1,000; the sale was completed on 2 December 1931. The new buildings, seven classrooms each holding forty pupils and an assembly hall, were finished in March 1932. The portable buildings were again re-used, this time being converted as a science laboratory and practical room.

By the late 1920s views about education were changing. A major influence was the report of the Hadow Committee on the Education of the Adolescent (1926) which viewed the education process in two stages, primary and secondary, with a break between the two at around the age of eleven. In line with the Hadow recommendations, the Essex County Council Education Committee had intended to reorganise its schools in the Upminster area into separate senior (secondary) mixed and junior mixed and infants with effect from September 1933. However, house building on the Gaynes Estate was still in its early stages and the recent electrification of the railway to Upminster and the opening of a station at Upminster Bridge looked likely to stimulate further growth in the area. The committee therefore decided that it would be necessary to buy sites for additional schools in the area and approval for the purchase from Mr A.E. Palmer of a 10 ½ acre site on the Cranston Park

Estate at a cost of £6,130 was given by the Board of Education on 26 January 1933. Four months later on 26 May 1933 the council issued public notices for the proposed senior school for 960 pupils from 'Upminster and the adjoining districts', including Cranham and North and South Ockendon.

Under the 1921 Education Act any ten or more ratepayers could raise objections to school building proposals announced in public notices. On 12 July 1933 Mr A. Rucker of 26 Cranston Park Avenue wrote to the Board of Education with a petition from nineteen other ratepayers, all in Cranston Park Avenue, objecting to the new school on four counts, claiming that:

- The new school wasn't needed.
- The existing 'Bell' School was better situated to meet the needs of the district.
- The proposed site was not accessible to most children.
- The erection of the school would cause a depreciation in property prices locally.

As a result of these objections the Board of Education was now required to examine in detail the county council's plans, together with their response to the ratepayers' objections. The Board's Inspectors and civil servants reached a number of important conclusions. They felt that the council would find it difficult to find another suitable site if the proposed one were lost, while the recent and expected growth in pupil numbers meant that the need for a new school was soundly established. However, the council's proposal for a school with 960 places was not supported: the Board felt that by the time the county council had erected the school – a minimum of 18 months, no earlier than April 1935 – numbers would 'go a long way towards filling a school for 480 pupils', only half the proposed size. The county were therefore told to submit revised plans for a 480 pupil school; this was done on New Years Day 1934. As pupil numbers continued to rise rapidly, pending the building of the new senior school, the council had no alternative but to convert the old Boys' School, then only used for practical lessons, back to full-time classrooms for two years from September 1934.

At the end of January 1935 the county council accepted the tender from Mr C. Deaves for £23,619 for the building of the new school and, as expected, building work took up most of the next eighteen months. In the meantime Mr Sidney Young, headmaster of Newport School, Essex was appointed head-master of Gaynes Senor Mixed School. In 1935 he visited 'The Bell School' to talk to the staff, offering posts at Gaynes to Mr F. Gordon Lacey, who became deputy head and art teacher, Mr Douglas Westrop, in later years to serve as Gaynes' headteacher, and Mr H. Jackman. The new school opened on 3 September 1936 with 399 pupils organised in eleven classes, four in the first year, three second year classes, and four in the third (top) year. In addition to the headteacher, there were twelve teachers, a domestic, a caretaker and two cleaners. The school colours were chosen as emerald green with gold piping with a badge designed by Mr Lacey featuring the windmill.

Naturally the first few weeks were hectic as the children got used to finding their way around the new buildings and adjusted to the differences to their previous schools. Those children from 'The Bell School' were used to a large school – but not one with two storeys – while those transferring from schools in North and South Ockendon had previously been taught in very small village schools; children from these districts were brought to school by coaches. Their new school had separate entrances and separate playgrounds for boys and girls and neither sex dared wander through the wrong gate or into the others' territory! The new school soon developed a strong musical tradition, and sport was also to the forefront, with many successes in local and county sports competitions. School trips were also popular including in May 1937 a visit by 100 children and 6 teachers to stay at East Cowes Holiday Camp on the Isle of Wight, where they were accommodated in wooden hutted dormitories.

The opening of Gaynes in September 1936 and the transfer of the top three year groups of children there considerably relieved pressure on The Bell. The county council could now go ahead with a reorganisation and the school was split into separate Infants and Junior mixed departments, as they still remain today. Finally in 1936 the Essex Education Committee declared that the British School premises were surplus to requirements and handed them back to the British School Trustees, who in March 1937 received the agreement of the Board of Education to sell the site, which fetched £6,400 at public auction later that year. (After delays of many years in 1951 the proceeds were used to establish the 'Old British School Foundation', a fund administered by trustees, for educational purposes which benefit children and young people resident in Upminster). Demolition of the British School began in January 1938, although shops were not built on this site until after World War Two.

At the same time that the county council had outlined the plans for Gaynes, they had recognised the need for additional junior school accommodation in the Upminster area to cater for the growing population. In December 1932 the county authority alerted the Board of Education to the need for another school, receiving the go-ahead to buy a site two months later. In May 1933 agreement was reached with Gaynes Park Estates to buy land with a frontage of 540ft in Cedar Avenue for £1850 for future use as a school; in July 1934 the site was fenced at a cost of £335. Work on the new school was planned to begin just before the outbreak of hostilities in 1939 and Branfill County Infants School opened in 1943 as a temporary school for 100 infants. From the same time Hornchurch County High School used the main part of the buildings, and the school was later described as 'the only secondary school in England to be built during the war'. The High School remained there until alternative premises

Class 1B at the newly opened Gaynes School in 1936 with their teacher Miss E. Grinter.

(now Emerson Park School) were built off Wingletye Lane, Hornchurch in 1954, at which time the vacated premises became Branfill Junior School.

Another part of Upminster's educational jigsaw came with the development of St Joseph's Roman Catholic Primary School. This opened just after the war in Mavisbank, which had been used as the Presbytery until the new church of St Joseph and adjacent priest's house were completed in 1939. Initially the school provided 110 places and was an annexe to St Mary's Primary School, Hornchurch, recognised by the Ministry of Education in 1953. With the demolition of Mavisbank in September 1956, the new voluntary aided school of St Joseph's was built on the vacated site.

11

UPMINSTER SURVIVALS

UPMINSTER WINDMILL

UPMINSTER'S WINDMILL IS possibly the area's best known, best loved and almost certainly the most photographed landmark in the parish. Indeed it has been said by the historian of Essex windmills that 'more words have been written about Upminster windmill than any other in Essex'. Yet for some years this 200-year-old structure lacked attention and had an uncertain future. But for the interest of local residents it could easily have met the same fate as other familiar Upminster buildings, destroyed from the 1930s onwards, and its site could now have been covered with housing.

'Strong presumptive evidence from the parish rate books', along with other evidence, dates the mill to the autumn of 1803, the initiator being James Nokes of Hunts Farm and later of Bridge House Farm. This smock mill built in the Kentish style was a parallel enterprise to another mill which the Nokes family had built earlier on the West Thurrock waterfront. Standing in a prominent position overlooking the Ingrebourne valley to the west, Nokes' Upminster mill was well placed to make good use of the prevailing wind, with Hornchurch's post mill visible on the opposite ridge.

The Upminster mill was a very early example of the introduction of steam power in milling, and was possibly the earliest such usage in Essex, which Wilson dated to May 1811. James Nokes died in 1838 and was succeeded by his brother Thomas, who in turn died in 1846. James's son Thomas then took over but three years later in 1849 after his bankruptcy he sold the mill, two millers' cottages and a millpond to Ambrose Colson for £2,000, who soon sold the property privately to James Weyman Wadeson. In September 1857 Wadeson agreed to sell the windmill and land to Thomas Abraham, the sale finally being completed on 23 July 1859. Abraham, born in the year the mill was built, had been Nokes' foreman at the mill in 1844 and again foreman there in 1851. He tried his hand at farming and raised sufficient capital to pay

Upminster windmill 1908. At this time the mill was still in working order.

Wadeson £1,100 for the mill and 12 acres of adjoining land. In two or three years Thomas had restored the mill's fortunes, which had declined under the previous management and the following decades were the prime years when the business flourished. Thomas Abraham's elder son, also named Thomas, was not interested in continuing the milling trade and on Thomas senior's death in 1882 the business passed to his younger son John Arkell Abraham.

In the course of a severe thunderstorm in September 1889, during which 4in. of rain fell in seven hours, the mill was struck by lightning which cut a sail to pieces and fused the sack-chain links. Just over ten years later at the end of December 1899 worse damage occurred during a gale when the massive cast-iron shaft supporting the sails, snapped, sending the sails crashing to the ground where the were smashed to pieces, damaging part of the lower stage as they fell. Replacing the sails was not strictly necessary, as the mill was in any event powered by steam and only occasionally worked by wind. But the villagers, fearing the loss of their picturesque landmark, rallied round to contribute £150 towards the £200 cost of repair, enabling a post-mill windshaft from a mill at Maldon to be installed.

John Arkell Abraham died in July 1912, aged eighty-one. By his will his three nephews, Thomas, Alfred and Clement Abraham, sons of his brother Thomas who died in 1897, inherited 'the goodwill of his trade as a miller'. They ran the mill and the related coal merchant's business as T., A. & C. Abraham. John Arkell Abraham also devised the rest of his estate to these three, and their other two brothers Ernest Abraham of Walthamstow and Sidney Abraham, baker of Station Road, who soon sold their shares to the other three. However, the venture was increasingly uneconomic, particularly due to the effects of the First World War which meant there was less corn to grind and the mill was under-used. By the winter of 1926/27 the windmill was not in use and when a strong wind on 25 March 1927 ripped the fan off the mill, there was some doubt that it was worthwhile to put it back in working order. After the death of Clement, the business manager, on 3 September 1935 the remaining two brothers Thomas and Alfred offered the mill for sale in December 1935 (Thomas died shortly afterwards while Alfred, a familiar figure in Upminster still remembered as a Sunday School teacher, survived to the age of ninety-five, dying in 1959).

The purchaser was William Henry Simmons of The Lord Stanley, Plaistow (and later of 7 Highview Gardens, Upminster) who paid £3,400 for the property, but in May 1937 Simmons himself offered the mill for sale. Members of the windmill section of the Society for the Protection of Ancient Buildings attempted to buy the mill but the price was beyond their means. The Society expressed concerns over the disappearance of Essex windmills and in July 1937 Essex County Council, prompted by the possibility that the mill would be demolished and houses built on the site, decided that in view of its special historic and architectural interest the mill should not be demolished without their consent. Five months later in December 1937 Hornchurch Urban District Council asked the county authority to consider moving the mill and 're-erecting it on a more suitable site' – they felt that a site hemmed in by houses was inappropriate.

> The local Council's proposal to relocate the mill prompted the following poem in the *Hornchurch and Upminster News*:
>
> They wish to pull down the old windmill
> They want to move it and we think they will
> But what will they do if they can't find a view
> That's as good as the one on the hill?

It seems that Essex County Council entered negotiations with Simmons with the aim of buying the mill. By October 1938 sufficient progress had been evidently made for Essex County Council to agree to grant Hornchurch UDC a 999-year lease on the mill site for a nominal rent, with the aim of relieving the county of future maintenance costs. In March 1939 before handing over the mill to Hornchurch the county council decided to spend £152 on repairs. By May 1939 Essex County Council had reached agreement with Simmons on the arrangements for buying the mill itself, and the right to gain access from St Mary's Lane. The rest of the site, including a proposed housing development on the west side to be known as 'Windmill Close', was to stay in Simmons' ownership. But Simmons died the following month in June 1939 and the proposed sale was delayed, finally going ahead in January 1940 for the agreed price of £475 with the agreement of Simmons' executors.

The mill in about 1949 when it was badly in need of restoration.

Meanwhile the county council found that the district council were not empowered to incur costs in running the windmill so the plans to lease the mill to them were dropped. War led to immense pressure on building materials and the county council were unable to obtain the building licence needed to carry out repairs. As a result the property suffered considerable decay during the war years, a survey in 1946 estimating the cost of repair at £400.

With the ending of war in 1945 efforts were made by Hector Stone, a retired Suffolk miller, to revive the mill as a working machine but to no avail. In August 1946 a public meeting was called to discuss the condition of the windmill, arising from which a Windmill Committee was formed to raise funds to carry out the needed repairs, backed by the Society for the Protection of Ancient Buildings. In August 1949 a tenancy agreement for the mill as a nominal 1s was signed between Essex County Council and Howard Frizzell, James Francis, Ronald Hewitson and Charles Marriner as trustees of the Windmill Committee. The committee organised a programme of restoration work to be carried out by volunteers working in their own time, and fundraising efforts allowed some repairs to be done in 1949 under the supervision of Hector Stone. By May 1950 a new body known as the Friends of the Mill had been formed for the purpose of raising funds and maintaining the mill, under which for an annual subscription of 5s members would have access to the mill for themselves and their guests. But public enthusiasm soon waned and by 1958 it was noted that 'battens drop, boards fall off and machinery, made by skilled and careful hands, is smashed by hooligans and thieves'. The out-buildings were then 'desolate', the old garden 'a barren wilderness' and 'the house and cottages mere skeletons'. The situation appeared so bad that the decay 'if unchecked, is bound sooner or later to make restoration impossible'.

In May 1960, after years of negotiations and some twenty years after acquiring the mill, the county authorities finally bought the rest of the still-undeveloped site from Simmons' executors for £3,650 – a purchase price of £1,250 and an 'established development value' of £3,400. Essex County Council then spent £4,000 demolishing the near-derelict mill house, steam plant and out-buildings and levelling the site. In 1962/63 they undertook major repairs and maintenance to the mill itself at a cost of £2,000, making the building weather- and vandal-proof. With the formation of the London Borough of Havering in April 1965, the ownership of the mill finally passed from the county council to the local authority. There was a revival in local interest and involvement which finally now ensured the mill's preservation, and in 1967 the windmill was opened to the public on a regular basis, thanks to the voluntary efforts of the Hornchurch and District Historical Society. The Society continues to fulfil an important function by opening the premises to visitors on summer weekends.

INGREBOURNE COTTAGES

Ingrebourne Cottages stand on the north side of St Mary's Lane, just east of the Bridge House Inn (now the Hungry Horse) and at the foot of Upminster Hill, opposite the junction with Bridge Avenue. Dating from 1750 and extended in 1786 many people still pass these, unaware that until 1836 the cottages formed the workhouse for the parish of Upminster.

The workhouse's origins arose in an Act of 1722 which allowed par-ishes to build or lease houses to accommodate their poor. The Branfills of Upminster Hall had invested £100 at 4% per annum for this purpose and the land, 'part of the waste soil of the Manor', was granted to the churchwardens at a yearly rent of 2s 6d. Although the Vestry had decided in 1741 to proceed with plans for the workhouse, work did not take place until 1750. Edward Sumpner, bricklayer, and John Badger, carpen-ter, of Hornchurch were the main tradesmen who carried out the nec-essary building work. Within a few decades increasing pauper numbers meant that some had to be boarded out at Warley. The workhouse was therefore extended in 1786, Samuel Hammond carrying out the work for some £179.

With the formation of Poor Law Unions, under which from 1835 Upminster was grouped with many other neighbouring parishes to form the Romford Poor Law Union, Upminster's poor were thereafter accommodated at the Romford Union Workhouse at Oldchurch Road. No longer needed, Upminster's parish workhouse was sold for £356 to George Rowe who converted the property into six terraced cottages, which still remain today. Although hardly a major historical monument the buildings, classified as Grade II listed, have played an important role in Upminster's history.

CORBETS TEY ROAD

Still standing on Corbets Tey Road (No. 201) opposite Little Gaynes Lane, the building known as Gaynes Cross betrays little hint of its history. Probably built around 1770 this was a former lodge of Gaynes Manor, marking the eastern approach. The lodge at Gaynes Cross marked the site of the manorial pound where stray animals were placed until claimed by their owners. Another lodge, known as West Lodge or Gaynes Lodge, stood on Little Gaynes Lane near the western entrance to Gaynes Park and housed the estate's coachman.

The house now known as Tadlows, still surviving as 251 Corbets Tey Road, also formed part of the manor of Gaynes. On three floors, the house has six bedrooms, two living rooms and two kitchens, no doubt reflecting the fact that the property was split into two dwellings for sometime at the start of the twentieth century. The first house on the site certainly predated 1704, in which year it was named 'Rolfs' and held by Mrs Susannah Latham. In 1720 it was known as Peacock's and the farmhouse and surrounding fields were later added to Sir James Esdaile's extensive landholdings. Esdaile is believed to have rebuilt the house in its current form around 1770. The house takes its name from Mr Tadlow, a former occupier who in 1790 during Esdaile's ownership of Gaynes, superintended the work in which the stream which flowed from Cranham through Gaynes Park was dug up and widened into the lake which still survives in Parkland Open Space (the earth taken out was distributed around the park). A later owner was James Nokes, builder of Upminster Mill.

Upminster, Gaynes Cross.

Gaynes Cross, still surviving opposite Little Gaynes Lane, was the eastern lodge for Great Gaynes. This picture dates from 1908.

Reunited with Gaynes Manor by Rev. George Clayton, Tadlows was used to house employees of the estate. An occupier of half of the house immediately before Joslin's death in 1927 was Jonathan Hills, Joslin's gardener at Gaynes, while the other was occupied by Richard Stokes, Joslin's Foreman. At that time the farm comprised just over 81 acres, lying south of what became Park Drive, eastwards from Corbets Tey Road. It was developed by A.D. MacGregor as the Cranston Park Estate.

CORBETS TEY AND SOUTHERN UPMINSTER

More so than elsewhere in the parish of Upminster, the area around Corbets Tey village still retains enough rural charm to recall the days when Upminster still justified its title of 'an Essex beauty spot'. Approaching Corbets Tey from the west along Harwood Hall Lane the view differs little from that in the early years of the twentieth century: on the south side stand a row of eight cottages (Nos. 1 to 8 Harwood Hall Lane) in the Essex weatherboard style. Once known as Bearblock Cottages, after a former owner, Nos. 1 to 3 were once a single house of the early seventeenth century, divided when the adjacent Nos. 4 to 8 were built in the mid-eighteenth century. Beyond them, close to the junction with Corbets Tey Road, is the old Anchor, which until 1896 was one of three inns in the hamlet of Corbets Tey. In 1891 the Anchor

A scene from 1908 that remains much the same today – the view looking up Harwood Hall Lane towards Corbets Tey village.

was listed as the home of Eliza Manklow, grocer and beer retailer; she was the widow of John Manklow and daughter of Benjamin and Eliza Phillips who had moved to Corbets Tey from Deptford around 1868. In the first half of the twentieth century it was the home of Mr J.W. Gunnell, chairman of Upminster Parish Council.

High House, Corbets Tey from the rear, *c.* 1912.

Adjacent to the old Anchor and standing opposite Corbets Tey Road is High House, not to be confused with the former house of the same name which stood opposite St Laurence's church. With a fine view which once looked directly towards Gaynes Manor, this narrow house has a brick façade dating from the late 1600s, and lower timber-framed wings from an earlier era. It has a well-documented history and for a long period at the start of the nineteenth century was used as a boarding school, originally by a Mr Saunders who was exempt from service in the Napoleonic Wars due to a withered arm. Bought with 28 acres of land in the 1860s by Richard Clark and used as a market garden, the Clark family remained there until 1950, at which time water was still obtained from a pump in the kitchen.

The present Huntsman and Hounds pub was reopened on 28 May 1896, about 20 yards east and some 10ft further from the road than the former building which it replaced, demolished in October 1895 and dating from the

The old Huntsmen & Hounds, Corbets Tey. When the current building was opened in 1896 the spelling of the name had changed to 'Huntsm*an*'.

eighteenth century. The owner Frank H Rowe, who had bought the premises in 1895, was prominent in local affairs, serving on the parish council.

Opposite on the corner of Corbets Tey Road and Ockendon Road is the Old Cottage, once an inn called The Royal George, later the George, and in 1835 listed as the George and Dragon. It ceased trading as a public house in October 1901 when the licence was transferred to Romford by the owners Ind Coope & Co., the last glass of beer being sold by the landlord Thomas Starr to William Snell, a local shoemaker. This timber-framed building, now probably over 300 years old, had an elaborate Jacobean fireplace until 1969.

Taking Ockendon Road leading east and making a brief detour southwards, the still-surviving Great Sullens (or Sunnings) Farm is reached, standing well back from the road on the east side of Sunnings Lane. Great Sullens is in the occupation of Mr Eric Knight, son of Jack Knight, who was a well-known local farmer and market gardener. One of the oldest farmhouses in Upminster, possibly dating back to the Elizabethan period, Wilson indicated that there was 'abundant evidence of its antiquity', although sadly Jacobean panelling and a fine Adam fireplace went to the USA after the last war. Sunnings was a place of some importance in the early years of the sixteenth century, during the reign of Henry VII (1485-1509). A century later Thomas Frith, founder of the principal parish charity, was the occupier until 1610 and two years later one of the trustees of Ralph Latham's estate, John Frith,

Harwood Hall, Corbets Tey, is another eighteenth-century house built by Esdaile.

scrivener of London, lived there. Alfred Abraham lived here before moving to the mill on the death in 1912 of John Arkell Abraham, while the Gay family were occupiers for many years in the early twentieth century. Little Sunnings on the other side of the road a little further along, which may be older still, is in the occupation of Mr Eric Knight, son of Jack Knight, who was a well-known local farmer and market gardener. Both Great and Little Sunnings are Grade II listed buildings.

Harwood Hall is another of the properties erected by Sir James Esdaile, built in 1790 for his son-in-law George Stubbs Esq., replacing an earlier house on the same site. Sir Thomas Barrett Lennard lived there from 1801 to 1804 after living at Hactons and before taking residence at nearby Belhus. The property and land was bought from the Esdaile family in 1819 by Philip Zachariah Cox, on whose death without issue in 1858 it passed, along with nearby High House, to A.Z. Button, who assumed the name of Cox. Colonel Henry Holmes Esq., owner of Hornchurch Brewery, lived here up to 1877 when his magnificent house of Grey Towers was built. Both houses were similar, and the battlements of Harwood Hall may well have been added during Holmes's tenancy or the style may have influenced the design for Grey Towers.

In the late nineteenth century and the first two decades of the twentieth century Harwood Hall was a popular venue for treats provided for the local children by the tenants, Herbert Platten and family. During the decades that followed the owners were William Grant Fiske, senior and junior, who also owned Londons.

Another survival in rural Upminster is Hactons, at the junction of Little Gaynes Lane and Hacton Lane, described by Wilson as 'a spacious and well-proportioned red brick building with stone quoins and dressings'. Built between 1762 and 1765 by William Braund, a successful Portugal merchant and city financier who lived in the house until his death in 1774, it was used by the army in the Second World War as a troop billet. Afterwards it remained unoccupied and it was discovered that trespassers were gaining access to the house from the grounds through an underground passage, now blocked up. In 1954 Hactons was considerably altered and converted to flats, the roof line of the main block being altered to provide windows for the attic storey.

UPMINSTER (TYLER'S) COMMON AND THE NORTH OF THE PARISH

The survival of Upminster's common, now restored to its proper name of Tyler's Common, did not occur by chance as confirmed by the stone celebrating the success in 1951 of a campaign to preserve this amenity. This common, containing 78 acres of grazing land on the east of Nag's Head Lane, was part of the manor of Upminster Hall (Gaynes Common, part of Gaynes Manor, was on the west side of Nag's Head Lane where Ivy Lodge Farm now is). Tyler's Common was requisitioned by the Essex War Committee during the Second World War for the growing of crops and in 1950 the county council tried to enclose the common for this purpose. Edward Luther and other local residents, with the backing of the Ministry of Agriculture, launched a strong and successful campaign which preserved the common for public access.

Great Tomkyns Farm, in the far north of the parish in Tomkins (formerly Bird) Lane, is certainly one of the oldest and possibly the finest in the area, described by Pevsner as 'a good 15th-century yeoman's house with exposed timber framing. The hall goes up to the whole height of the building. The wings to its west and east are two-storeyed'. In 1701 Andrew Branfill, owner of Upminster Hall Manor, gave Great Tomkyns to his daughter Elizabeth and her husband Harman Browse, a Stepney merchant. Along with Upminster Hall and the windmill, Great Tomkyns is one of only three Grade II listed buildings in the parish.

On the north-eastern fringes of Tyler's Common, just off Nag's Head Lane, near to the parish boundary stands Tyler's Hall, a weather-boarded farmhouse dating from the eighteenth century. The time Tyler's is probably a corruption of 'Tigelhyrst', derived from two words signifying a wood providing earth for making tiles; the farmland was probably enclosed from the adjacent common. Like Great Tomkyns Tyler's Hall was also the home of one of Andrew Branfill's daughters, Mary and her husband Capt. John Redman, whose pocketbook survives in the Essex Record Office. The farm remained in the ownership of the descendents of the Redman family well into the twentieth century.

Another farmhouse of some antiquity is Page's Farm approached from Shepherd's Hill but just in Upminster. Named after the Page family, farmers there from the start of the eighteenth century, the farm is extensively altered and has smoke-blackened rafters in the central roof section, with the date 1663 carved on a corbel supporting a great oak beam on the ground floor.

And finally, on this whistle-stop description of Upminster survivals, is what we now know as the Tithe Barn in Hall Lane, which has become a well-known feature of this parish since its restoration and conversion into an agricultural and rural life museum opened on summer weekends since 1976 by the Hornchurch and District Historical Society. However, this was not always the case. There is no mention of this building in 1958 in Books 2 and 3 of *The Story of Upminster,* which describe the parish's historic buildings. Some years later Valerie Body described the barn in *The Upminster Story* as 'much patched with corrugated iron over the years and [it] does not look very picturesque'.

There is also no evidence that despite its currently-accepted title it was ever a barn used to stock the rector's tithes and it is more likely that it was originally a barn used by nearby Upminster Hall. Now thatched, this nine-bayed, timber-framed barn possibly dates to as early as 1450, although it could date 200 years later, during Ralph Latham's ownership of the manor. It was separated from the Upminster Hall estate in 1935 and bought by Hornchurch UDC, along with the adjacent 30 acres of lands which now form Hall Lane Playing Fields, passing into Havering Council's ownership in 1965.

Upminster or Tyler's Common only survived after a strong public campaign.

CHRONOLOGY OF UPMINSTER

1851	28 February	Opening of the British School.
	25 March	Opening of the National School.
	30 March	Population of Upminster is 1,228
1861	7 April	Population of Upminster is 1,342
	June	Major rebuilding of St Laurence church begins to Bartleet's design.
1862	1 March	St Laurence church reopens for worship.
1870	January	Rev. Alfred Morgan Carter takes over ministry at the Congregational church.
1871	2 April	Population of Upminster is 1,342
1873		Hill Place rebuilt to Bartleet's design.
	September	Congregational chapel on Upminster Hill enlarged. Manse built opposite chapel.
1877		George Frederick West takes over as master of National School.
1881	January	T.L. Wilson's *History of Upminster* completed.
	3 April	Population of Upminster is 1,202
1882		Windmill on Upminster (Gaynes) Common taken down.
1883	11 October	First turf cut at Upminster for Barking to Pitsea railway extension.
1885	30 January	School Board established after managers of National and British Schools agree to merger.
	1 May	Opening of L.T. & S. Railway to Upminster.

	21 June	Formal merger of British and National Schools under School Board.
	September	Schools re-organised to form Boys' School in former National School building, and Girls' and Infants' School in British School building.
1888	April	British School building extended.
	2/3 August	River Ingrebourne overflows; Bridge House deluged and bridge dangerous for heavy traffic.
1891	5 April	Population of Upminster is 1,409
1892	9 January	New Bridge over the River Ingrebourne, twice width of former bridge.
	1 July	Opening of railway from Upminster to Grays.
	December	E. Sydney Woodiwiss purchases Hill Place and sets up private zoo.
1893		Cockabourne Bridge rebuilt by Essex County Council, with contributions from parish.
	7 June	Opening of railway from Upminster to Romford.
1894	17 December	Upminster's first parish council elected.
1896	May	The famous cricketer W.G. Grace stays at Hill Place.
	28 May	Huntsman & Hounds, Corbets Tey reopens in new premises.
1901		Ten-acre Mavisbank estate acquired for development by Davis & Dowsing of Romford.
	April	Population of Upminster is 1,477
1902	9 May	The cemetery Corbets Tey opened.
1904		Work on Mavisbank estate (Branfill Park) begins. Branfill, Gaynes and Champion Roads begun. H.H. Holden succeeds Philip M. Holden as rector.
1905	March	Building of Upminster Court for A.E. Williams commences to Charles Reilly's designs.
1906	September	W.P. Griggs announces proposals to develop Upminster Hall Estate.
	November	Work begins on first houses on Upminster Hall Estate.
1907	May	Press and others visit Upminster to view progress on Griggs' estate.
	November	Retirement of Rev. A.M. Carter of Congregational church.
1907/8		Station Road shops built & opened by April 1908.

Upminster Court, Hall Lane – the last great house built in Upminster.

1909	29 September	New Place Estate bought by W.P. Griggs & Co.
	October	Rev. Stanley Bloomfield ordained as Congregational church minister.
	1 October	Emerson Park Halt opens on Upminster-Romford line.
1910	July	Methodist church opens in 'Tin Tabernacle' in Hall Lane.
1911		Westminster Bank built on corner of Branfill & Station Road.
		Plymouth Brethren re-open old Congregational chapel
	29 March	New Congregational church opened in Station Road.
1913	March	Death of James Roome, founder of Roomes Stores.
	November	Essex County Council agree to buy 22 acres of land, formerly part of New Place, as a site for a new council school.
1914	August	St Laurence Hall opened (following outbreak of war re-equipped as an auxiliary war hospital).
1917		Death of Rev. A.M. Carter, former Congregational minister.
1919	June	Death of T.L. Wilson, Upminster's historian.

1920	August	Death at Ilford of Sir W. Peter Griggs, MP.
	September	Congregational church war memorial tablet unveiled.
1921		Development of New Place estate begins.
	April	Population of Upminster is 3,559.
	7 May	War memorial unveiled by Major-General Rougemont.
1922		Temporary Catholic church opens at junction of Sunnyside Gardens.
	22 July	Hornchurch Road & Cranham Lane renamed St Mary's Lane.
	November	Death of John Wilson, last tenant of New Place.
		Telephone exchange opened over Greens Stores.
1923		Negotiations & debate about purchase by parish council of New Place and Clockhouse.
	February	Foundation stone laying for Commemoration Hall, Congregational church.
	2 February	Foundation stone of new Methodist church in Hall Lane laid.
1924	June	New Place demolished.
1925		Elm tree by smithy cut down & fate of smithy sealed.
		Churchyard extended.
	25 March	Arterial Road (now A127) opened by Prince Henry, Duke of Gloucester.
1926	April	Hornchurch Rural District Council created.
	26 July	Public meeting at Bell agrees to form golf club
1927	March	'Bell' School opens in temporary (portable) buildings at St Mary's lane. Work on permanent school begins.
	5 March	Death of Mr Henry Joslin, DL JP, of Gaynes.
	April	First Roomes Stores shop opens in Station Road.
	2 May	Nuns of Sacred Heart Convent buy Hill Place from Dr J.S. Brookfield for use as a boarding and day schools for Catholic girls and infants.
1928	April	Permanent school 'The Bell' opens for 450 children in St Mary's Lane.
	26 May	Upminster Golf Club opened by Mr W.G. Key.
	5 June	Death of Charles Reilly of High House.
	July	New Police Station built in St Mary's Lane.
1929	11 April	Telephone exchange transfers from above Greens Stores (junction of Howard Road & Station Lane) to new site in St Mary's Lane.
	May	Work starts on Ford Motor Works at Dagenham.

	July	Auction to sell Gaynes Park Estate – many lots remain unsold.
	October	Ceremony to rededicate St Laurence church extensions.
	10 October	Opening of Capitol Cinema in St Mary's Lane.
	27 November	Purchase of Glebelands completed by parish council.
1930	October	Gaynes House demolished.
1931	April	Population of Upminster is 5,732
	November	Death of William Garbutt Key, Director of Upminster Estates Ltd.
1932	25 January	Subway joining 'up' and 'down' platforms closed to public.
	10 March	Bell School expanded – 7 classrooms and hall added.
	12 September	Opening of electrified District Line service between Barking and Upminster.
	3 December	Catholic church moves to temporary premises in wooden buildings in Champion Road.
1933		Brickworks close.
1934		Mavisbank bought by Catholic church.
	1 April	Upminster Parish Council becomes part of Hornchurch Urban District Council.
	August	Signpost at Bell Corner taken down.
	17 December	Upminster Bridge Station opened.
1935	18 July	High House sold by auction and later demolished.
	29 July	Stonelaying ceremony at Baptist Church, Springfield Gardens.
	September	Death of Clement Abraham leads to decision to sell windmill; purchased in December 1935 W.H. Simmons.
	21 November	Baptist church opens in Springfield Gardens.
1936	20 February	Hunts Farm sold by auction and later demolished.
	August	First shops in Byron Parade shops open on former High House site.
	1 September	Gaynes Secondary School opens.
	12 October	Part-time library opens in the Clockhouse.
1937		Tithe Barn and 30a bought by Hornchurch UDC.
	1 May	Extended Roomes store opened.
	July	Essex County Council grant preservation order on windmill.
	2 November	Chestnuts and Locksley Villas demolished.

The signpost at the Four Wantz Corner, outside the Bell, taken down August 1934.

1938		Gasometer at rear of Bridge House removed.
	10 January	British School demolished.
	6 May	Hoppey Hall sold to A.D. MacGregor.
	4 November	Burtons Store opens at Aggiss's (Chestnuts) Corner.
1939	16 January	Hoppey Hall demolished.
	31 January	Death of William Aggiss, founder of Chestnuts Garage.
	25 March	Foundation stone laid at St Joseph's R.C. church.
	31 March	Retirement of Dr Bletsoe after over 30 years as an Upminster GP; his house at junction of Branfill & Station Roads purchased by Roomes for future redevelopment.
	3 November	St Joseph's Catholic church, Champion Road opened by Bishop of Brentwood.
1940	16 January	Essex County Council buy Windmill from executors of W.H. Simmons.
1943		Hornchurch County High School and Branfill Infant School, Cedar Avenue opened.
1949	1 January	Windmill leased to Windmill Committee who start restoration appeal.
1950	8 December	Traffic lights at Bell Corner come into use.

1951	April	Population is 13,038
1954		Branfill Junior School opens; Hornchurch Grammar School transfers to site off Wingletye Lane.
1956		Corbets Tey Special School opens.
	September	Mavisbank demolished.
1957		Roomes furnishing store opens on site of former doctor's house.
		South Essex Crematorium opened at Corbets Tey.
	January	Cosy Corner shop demolished (site bought January 1956 by Hornchurch UDC).
1959	22 June	Corbets Tey smithy closed down.
1962	23 September	Bell Inn closed down and demolished December 1962.
1963		Library in Corbets Tey Road opened.
	February	Death of Albert Edward Talbot, founder of A.E. Talbot & Sons.
1967		National School demolished.
1972		Old Westminster Bank demolished.
1974		Former Capitol/Gaumont Cinema demolished.
1976		Tithe Barn opens as agricultural and folk museum.

The Bell Inn, October 1962, after its closure and a few months before its demolition.

BIBLIOGRAPHICAL NOTES

THERE HAVE OF course been a number of books about Upminster's past, starting with the first edition of Thomas Lewis Wilson's *History* in 1854. Each has contributed in some way, large or small, to this current work, namely:

History and Topography of Upminster, Thomas L Wilson (1881)
The Story of Upminster: a story of an Essex village, Upminster Local History Group:

Book 1	*A Short Walk Into History*	December 1957
Book 2	*Historic Buildings (1)*	February 1958
Book 3	*Historic Buildings (2)*	April 1958
Book 4	*People of the Middle Ages*	June 1958
Book 5	*The Branfills of Upminster Hall*	August 1958
Book 6	*The Windmill*	December 1958
Book 7	*The Manor of Gaynes*	February 1959
Book 8	*Church and Rectors*	June 1959
Book 9	*The Parish Workhouse*	November 1959
Book 10	*Roads, Bridges And Inns*	March 1960
Book 11	*Crime and Police*	September 1960
Book 12	*"The Good Old Days"*	December 1960
Book 13	*Victorian Upminster*	December 1961
Book 14	*The Development of Modern Upminster*	December 1962

The Upminster Story, Valerie A Body (1973)
Victoria County History of Essex Volume VIII (1983) *pages 143-163.*
Our Old Upminster and District, Ted Ballard (1980)
Our Old Romford and District, Ted Ballard (1981)
A History of Upminster and Cranham, John Drury (1986)
Bygone Hornchurch and Upminster, Brian Evans (1990)
Upminster and Hornchurch – a pictorial history, Brian Evans (1996)

Relevant articles have been referred to in the notes on specific chapters. Thomas Wilson's archive of scrapbooks (T/P 67/1-14) at the Essex Record Office (ERO), Chelmsford provide a major source for press cuttings, mainly from *Romford Times*, *Grays and Tilbury Gazette* and *Essex Times* from around 1880 to about 1919. In general, references to press reports are from this source. I was fortunate enough to have access to relevant title deeds for properties in Upminster, now owned by London Borough of Havering, and I would like to thank Mr Bob Brannon at Romford Town Hall for arranging for the appropriate documents to be made available for me to study.

CHAPTER 1 – THE COMING OF THE RAILWAYS

Ken Frost's booklet *The Romford-Upminster Branch* Signal Railway Papers (1964) pages 10-16 provides a detailed account of Upminster's railways and in particular the 1883 ceremony. The descriptions of the parish draw mainly on Wilson (1881) and *The Story of Upminster Book 1*. Details of the Branfill family's plans for development south of the railway are found at ERO D/F 8/474 (records of Chancellors, architects of Chelmsford).

CHAPTER 2 – LANES OF ELM AND OAK

Information on late Victorian and Edwardian housing and Ebenezer Howard and his garden city movement are drawn from a number of sources, including *The Middle Classes 1900-1950* by Alan A Jackson (1991) and the article "Housing and the Lower Middle Class, 1870-1914" by S Martin Gaskell in *The Lower Middle Class in Britain 1870-1914* edited by Geoffrey Crossick (1977) pages 159-183. A more detailed account of Sir Peter Griggs is found in my article "Sir Peter Griggs M P: a self-made man" in *Cockney Ancestor* (journal of the East of London Family History Society) 63, Summer 1994 pages 35-38; some outline details appear in *Semi-Detached London* by Alan A Jackson (1973). Details about progress on the finishing of the early roads on the estate are from the *Minutes of Romford Rural District Council* at Havering Reference Library, Romford. The *Membership Roll* of Upminster Congregational Church, kept at Trinity United Reform Church, provided information on some of the garden suburb's early migrants, and thanks are due to the late Hugh Drake for arranging access to this source.

CHAPTER 3 – A VILLAGE AT WAR

Wilson's scrapbooks at ERO provided the main source, supplemented by my own research in local newspapers for this period. Other useful details came from Charles T. Perfect's *Hornchurch during the Great War* (1920) and *First*

Things First: RAF Hornchurch and RAF Suttons Farm 1915-1962 by Eric Smith (1992). For a more detailed account of my research into Upminster's war dead see my articles "Upminster: Anatomy of a war memorial" and "Some corner of a foreign field: Clarence Sorrell" in *Cockney Ancestor, 57*, Winter 1993/94, pages 3-10.

CHAPTER 4 – HOMES FIT FOR HEROES

Useful background came from *The making of modern London 1914-1939* by Gavin Weightman and Steve Humphries (1984) and *Suburban Style: the British home, 1840-1960* by Helena Barrett and John Phillips (1987). Information about the setting up of Upminster Golf Club is from *Upminster Golf Club: the first fifty years 1928-1978* (1978) while details about Upminster Cricket Club are from *Upminster Cricket Club 1858-1958* (thanks are due to Keith Martin for the loan of this). Specific details are mainly from contemporary press reports in *Romford Times* or *Grays and Tilbury Gazette*.

CHAPTER 5 – GREAT GAYNES . . . BUT ALSO MANY LOSSES

This chapter is based on the unique knowledge of the late Albert Parish, supplemented by my own research in a range of sources, including the Electoral Registers (Romford Division) at ERO, Chelmsford. Various sale catalogues (High House, Hoppey Hall and "The Hollies"), a brochure for the Gaynes Park Estate and Gates and Son's *Residential Guide*, all loaned by Albert Parish, and brochures for Cranston Park Estate and Upminster Estates Ltd, provided by Mrs Ruth Davis, were also helpful. I am very grateful to Miss Madeline Salinger for providing information on the life and career of her late father, Alfred C Salinger.

CHAPTER 6 – HITLER V. UPMINSTER

This chapter owes much to Peter Watt's detailed description of the Havering area during the 1939-45 war in his *Hitler v Havering* (1994). My thanks to him for allowing me to draw on his research and details of Upminster war incidents. Although the press was subject to censorship, despite the omission of exact names and places in reports, the precise dates of incidents listed in Peter's book allow most of the relevant newspaper accounts to be traced. For the preparations for war the local newspapers also provide a running, usually critical, account of progress which I found fitted in usefully with the background information in Philip Zeigler's account in *London at war 1939-45* (1995). Albert Parish provided invaluable first-hand knowledge of Upminster incidents.

Chapter 7 – Station Road and its Traders – East Side

Albert Parish contributed significantly to this chapter, supplemented where necessary by my research into *Essex Post Office Directories*. Family details were kindly provided by Mrs Gladys Ellis née Talbot while Mrs Ruth Davis contributed a list of shopkeepers in the 1930s. Margaret Crabtree's recent recollections *Growing up in North Ockendon and Upminster* (1996) also provided some further details.

Chapter 8 – Station Road and its Traders – West Side

Again Albert Parish was a principal contributor but Mr John Roome also provided details about the Roome family and Roome's acquisition of properties and land, while Mr George Aggiss also helped by supplying information about the family business.

Chapter 9 – Church and Chapel

General background to the early church came from *Churches in the Landscape* by Richard Morris (1989). Wilson (1881) provides much useful information on the parish church and Congregational Chapel. Also helpful was: *The story of Upminster Book 8*; *The parish church of St Laurence, Upminster: a brief history and guide*; George Greenland's article "Upminster parish church: rebuilding 1862" in *Havering History Review*, 14 (1993); the article about William Derham – "Science on a shoestring" – by George Kissell in *Essex Countryside* (October 1957); *Twelve centuries of worship* Anthony D Butler; and *The story of Trinity* Dorothy Hutchison (1991).

Chapter 10 – Slates, Strokes and Pot-hooks

My understanding of the Victorian education system was helped by *A social history of education in England* by John Lawson and Harold Silver (1974). But a wealth of detail was provided by the Log Book for the British School (1871-1913), loaned to me by Albert Parish, and this was supplemented by information from the Board of Education files at Public Record Office, Kew (in particular ED21/28149, 28150 and 28151) and the minutes of the Education Committee of Essex County Council held at Havering Reference Library, Romford. Books and articles which proved useful were: *A short history of Gaynes School Upminster* compiled by Keith Bonny and Elizabeth Heath (1991); "How they hated the school board" by Dr Harold Priestley in *Essex Countryside* (July 1970); "Hill Place Upminster, its people and the convent school" by Janette Howell in *Havering History Review*, No.8 (September

1976); and an essay "School memories" by Dorothy Fairhead (ERO T/Z 25/213) written *c.*1957.

CHAPTER 11 – UPMINSTER SURVIVALS

Upminster windmill is well documented, with two booklets dealing solely with its history and functions, namely *The Story of Upminster Book 6* and *Upminster Windmill* by Anthony D Butler (1968). But this section also draws on my own original research in the local press and in the title deeds (No.1516) held by London Borough of Havering, which provided much new detail. The resulting section presents a different account of the mill to those previously provided. Also helpful was *Essex Windmills, millers and millwrights: Volume 5 parishes S-Z* by Kenneth G Farries. Other parts of this chapter have mainly been compiled from the previous written accounts.

FURTHER READING

Braintree & Bocking Through Time
John & Sandra Adlam
ISBN 978-1-84868-311-2

Available from all good bookshops or order direct from our website
www.amberleybooks.com